D0687703

THE FATHERS
OF THE CHURCH

A NEW TRANSLATION

VOLUME 63

THE FATHERS
OF THE CHURCH

A NEW TRANSLATION

ROY JOSEPH DEFERRARI
Editorial Director Emeritus

EDITORIAL BOARD

BERNARD M. PEEBLES
The Catholic University of America
Editorial Director

PAUL J. MORIN
The Catholic University of America
Managing Editor

ROBERT P. RUSSELL, O.S.A.
Villanova University

THOMAS P. HALTON
The Catholic University of America

†MARTIN R. P. McGUIRE
The Catholic University of America

WILLIAM R. TONGUE
The Catholic University of America

HERMIGILD DRESSLER, O.F.M.
The Catholic University of America

SR. M. JOSEPHINE BRENNAN, I.H.M.
Marywood College

MSGR. JAMES A. MAGNER
The Catholic University of America

REDMOND A. BURKE, C.S.V.
The Catholic University of America

IBERIAN FATHERS

VOLUME 2

BRAULIO OF SARAGOSSA
FRUCTUOSUS OF BRAGA

Translated by
CLAUDE W. BARLOW
Clark University
Worcester, Massachusetts

THE CATHOLIC UNIVERSITY OF AMERICA PRESS
Washington, D. C. 20017

NIHIL OBSTAT:

JOHN C. SELNER, S.S., S.T.D.
Censor Librorum

IMPRIMATUR:

✠PATRICK CARDINAL A. O'BOYLE, D.D.
Archbishop of Washington

January 22, 1969

The *nihil obstat* and *imprimatur* are official declarations that a book or pamphlet is free of doctrinal or moral error. No implication is contained therein that those who have granted the *nihil obstat* and the *imprimatur* agree with the content, opinions, or statements expressed.

Library of Congress Catalog Card No.: 70-80270
SBN #8132-0063-6

Copyright © *1969 by*
THE CATHOLIC UNIVERSITY OF AMERICA PRESS, INC.
All rights reserved

281.4

B258i

vi 2

169251

CONTENTS

v

Mills College Library
Withdrawn
MILLS COLLEGE
LIBRARY

WRITINGS OF
BRAULIO OF SARAGOSSA

INTRODUCTION

ST. BRAULIO IS CONCEDED by all to have been the best writer in Spain at the middle of the seventh century and second only to Isidore in all of Visigothic literature. The sources for the facts of his life are, in addition to his own works, some letters from Isidore, included in the present translation; some poems of his close associate Eugene II, later Bishop of Toledo;[1] also a chapter in the biographical work *On Famous Men* by Ildefonse.[2] The earliest full biography of Braulio was written in the thirteenth century, is full of fanciful stories composed for propaganda, and must be disregarded in a genuine historical account.[3]

Braulio was of an illustrious family, born probably about 585 to 590, most likely in Osma or Saragossa, though occasionally he shows a special knowledge of ecclesiastical customs in Gerona. It is known that his father, Gregory, was a bishop; hence, he may have been the Bishop of Osma of that name. Braulio had an older brother, John, born about 580, long a resident of Saragossa and bishop there from 619 until his death in 631. There was another brother, Fronimian, abbot of the monastery of St. Emilian in the Rioja. Braulio had a sister, Pomponia, who was an abbess, and a sister, Basilla, the wife of a nobleman. He refers to both of his brothers as his teachers and appears to have outlived all of his family with the possible exception of Fronimian.

---

1 F. Vollmer, ed., "Eugenii Toletani episcopi carmina," *Monumenta Germaniae Historica, Auct. Ant.* 14 (Berlin 1915) 229-91.
2 Ildephonsi episcopi Toletani *De viris illustribus* 12 (PL 96.195-206).
3 C. H. Lynch, *Saint Braulio, Bishop of Saragossa (631-651): His Life and Writings* (Washington 1938) 7-8.

Braulio's first formal education may have been with his father, and it was apparently continued under his brother John, who by 610 was superior of the monastery of the Eighteen Martyrs near Saragossa. While in his twenties, Braulio spent several years with Isidore in the religious school conducted by that famous savant in Seville. The close relation and affection between these two is indicated in letters of theirs which have been preserved. The exact date at which Braulio left Seville and returned to Saragossa to serve as archdeacon under his brother John is one of the points disputed by modern scholars, but I am inclined to follow almost completely the chronology set up by Msgr. C. H. Lynch, according to which Braulio left Seville in 619 or 620.[4] He returned to Saragossa for the rest of his life; for, upon the death of John in 631, he was himself made bishop there, an office which he held nearly 20 years. His death is now placed in 651 and probably on March 26 of that year, since that is the date of his commemoration.

Letters

The *Letters* of Braulio, which now form the most important part of his literary testament, were late in coming to the knowledge of the general public. They survived in a single manuscript, no. 22 in the Capitular Library of León, written in Spain in the ninth century. Only the few letters exchanged between Isidore and Braulio (1-6 and 8) were known from Isidorian manuscripts. The León manuscript was copied by Carlos Espinós, archivist there from 1741 to 1777, and one of the copies went to Manuel Risco, who was continuing

---

4 Lynch, *op. cit.*, is the only book in English on this Spanish writer. The more recent edition of the *Letters* of Braulio by Madoz has revealed that the earlier edition used by Lynch did not follow exactly the order of the letters in the manuscript, but, except for a few details, the reconstruction which Lynch set up may be used in its entirety. As frequent references will show, I have been constantly indebted to Msgr. Lynch's thorough and accurate scholarship.

Florez' series *España Sagrada*. Thus, the complete correspondence of Braulio had its first edition in that series.[5] Risco changed the order of several of the letters to restore them, as he thought, to exact chronological order. Risco's edition was repeated in PL 80.655-700. A new critical edition made from the manuscript was published by J. Madoz,[6] and it is, in general, the latter that is followed for the present translation.

No complete translation of the *Letters* of Braulio has been published in any language, so far as I have been able to discover. Madoz prints as a sample[7] a Spanish version of three of the letters from an Escorial manuscript. They are more often paraphrase than translation, as they usually avoid all the admitted difficulties of Braulio's text. I have relied heavily upon the interpretation, and occasionally the translation, of the numerous selections made by Lynch, which I judge amount to less than one-fifth of the complete text, but which do include all of the most informative passages. There is no study of the language of Braulio and the dictionaries are inadequate in covering his vocabulary, for I have compiled quite a list of Latin words of which I can find no example anywhere else in the language. It is enough to state that Braulio's writing is often "vexingly obscure"[8] and that I

---

5 *España Sagrada* 30 (Madrid 1774) 318-92.—The *Letters* of Braulio are entered at no. 1230 in Dekkers, *Clavis patrum latinorum*.

6 (Madrid 1941); unfortunately this new edition has more than 60 misprints and it has been necessary to check the whole of Risco's text. Further, Madoz does not apparently give a complete collation of the manuscript, which is still very much needed. Madoz indicates fully the exact order of the letters in the manuscript, but regretfully decided not to change the order established in the first edition. He made some corrections in the chronology, a few of which I have adopted; but his greatest contribution has been in studying the sources and formation of the letters. A beginning in the study of the language of Braulio has been made by Luis Riesco, "Aportaciones al estudio del 'que' romanico," *Emerita* 30 (1962) 273-80. He notes the tendency of Latinists to neglect Spanish Latin written after 600 A.D., and demonstrates the colloquialisms that can be found in Braulio, whose initial and concluding sentences only tend to be stylized. Elsewhere, he is never free of colloquialisms.

7 Pp. 209-12.

8 In the language of Prof. Charles J. Bishko.

do not hope to have solved all of the difficulties and puzzles therein. A new edition of the complete works of Braulio has been promised by Galindo, who translated into Spanish the whole of Lynch's book with some extra material in Appendices.[9]

The literary sources with which Braulio was acquainted have been studied by Madoz,[10] who has listed several passages from St. Augustine and St. Gregory the Great which Braulio adapted for his own use, and a truly impressive number of selections from St. Jerome, whose subject matter was extensively employed in the *Letters*. Braulio's copy of Jerome's *Letters* must have been well studied and worn. References to these passages have been included in the notes, insofar as they appeared significant. I have added one large quotation from Pope Leo the Great. There are, undoubtedly, many more such identifications that will be made in the future. In general, Braulio does not copy slavishly, but employs the ideas of his sources and rephrases them to suit his own convenience.

The *Letters* of Braulio which have been preserved were not written previous to his becoming Bishop of Saragossa in 631, except for perhaps the first three, which concern Isidore. There is a good spread over the twenty years during which Braulio held office; there are letters from his friends as well as to them, and there is a considerable variety of subject matter. Madoz classifies the letters in four groups. (1) The familiar letters include those to Isidore at the beginning of the collection and letters to other bishops and associates in religion, nos. 9, 10, 11, 13, 16, 23, 24, 25, 26, 27. (2) A second group is also to religious associates, but may be distinguished by discussion of religious questions rather than personal banter, nos. 12, 14, 22, 42, 43, 44, and the fragment from Tajo. (3) A distinct group, written to console relatives and friends on the

---

9 C. H. Lynch y P. Galindo, *San Braulio, Obispo de Zaragoza (631-51), Su Vida y sus Obras* (Madrid 1950).
10 *Gregorianum* 20 (1939) 407-22.

loss of loved ones, includes nos. 15, 18, 19, 20, 28, 29, 30, 34. (4) Finally, there are the letters which concern ecclesiastical affairs, of which one is to Pope Honorius and eight come from the correspondence with King Receswinth, nos. 17, 21, 31, 32, 33, 37, 38, 39, 40, 41.

These *Letters* represent the most complete documentation that has been preserved from this period concerning the Church and society in Spain. In addition to the King and to Eugene, known already for his poems, and to Tajo, who has left a few letters of his own, we have the names of more than twenty men and women of the period and we know enough to allow each of them to appear momentarily before our vision as individuals, while Braulio himself is revealed in all his wide concern, caring for the individual interests of members of his flock and the broader problems of the Church.

Life of St. Emilian

The reputation of Braulio previous to the eighteenth century was based primarily on his biographical account of a saint who had died a few years before his own birth. Emilian was born in 474 and lived almost to his one hundredth birthday. Most of his life was spent in the region of La Rioja, where now is located the famous monastery of San Millán de la Cogolla. It is not known exactly why Braulio and his two brothers were personally interested in St. Emilian, but John had dedicated the new basilica of Saragossa to Emilian's memory and Fronimian was apparently the contemporary successor of Emilian as Abbot of San Millán. Braulio's account in the introduction tells us that John had urged him to write the biography and had provided him with sufficient notes from the testimony of living persons who had known Emilian. Distraction of affairs and a temporary misplacing of the notes left the *Life* unfinished before John died, but a chance discovery of the notes inspired Braulio to finish the biography and dedicate it to Fronimian. A manuscript seen at San Millán two hundred years ago was said to have a subscription carrying a date in the Spanish era equivalent to A.D. 636, and this is generally accepted as the year in which the biography was completed.

There are two rival schools identifying the places referred to in the biography, but I have adopted with confidence the identifications given by Lynch.[11]

The *Life* was already known in Spain before Braulio died, for Fructuosus asked him for a copy.[12] At least nine manuscripts are now preserved in Spain and Portugal, six of them in Madrid. The first edition was in a work on Spanish monasteries by Prudencio de Sandoval, published in 1601, with the text in Section II, ff. 3-10, and a Castilian translation on ff. 10-18. The text with the widest circulation was that printed by Tamayo de Salazar in the middle of the seventeenth century.[13] I know of no versions in any language other than these two made in Spain. The present translation is based on the text of the more modern edition by L. Vasquez de Parga.[14]

List of the Books of Isidore

Another work of Braulio for which he was known during the Middle Ages is a very brief one containing a list of the

11 *Op. cit.* 231-55.
12 Letter 43 *infra.*—On the *Life*, see Socii Bollandiani, *Bibliotheca hagiographica latina* (Subsidia hagiographica 6; Brussels 1898-1901) no. 100.
13 Reprinted first in Mabillon, *Acta Sanctorum Ordinis S. Benedicti* and from that in PL 80.699-714, where it is most accessible today. I have also used Minguella's book on San Millán de la Cogolla; here the text is mostly the same as that in Sandoval, but the accompanying Spanish translation discusses many of the difficult passages, and has been extremely helpful.
14 *Vita S. Emiliani* (Madrid 1943), the first text to be based on a complete collation of all the manuscripts. I have also preserved, in part, the rather awkward numeration of chapters and sections found in all the editions. The most recent critical edition is in Ignazio Cazzaniga, "La vita di S. Emiliano, scritta da Braulione Cesaraugustano," *Bollettino del Comitato per la preparazione delle edizioni nazionali dei classici greci e latini* (Rome 1955) n.s., fasc. 2.

writings of Isidore and an even briefer eulogy of his friend. It was intended as an addition to Isidore's book *On Famous Men*, and is always found in the manuscripts, accompanying that book. The title which has become standard from printed editions of the sixteenth century and later is *Praenotatio librorum D. Isidori,* but apparently no manuscripts actually have the word *Praenotatio.* Appendix III of Galindo's translation of Lynch[15] contains the Latin text of this work as found in León manuscript 22, the same codex which contains the only copy of Braulio's *Letters.* Galindo gives sufficient reasons to indicate beyond doubt that *Renotatio* rather than *Praenotatio* was the title provided either by Braulio himself or by an editor after his death. The work is surely a new list of the writings of Isidore, compiled after his death, rather than advance notice of those works.

There are seventeen titles in Braulio's list, each accompanied by a description in a single sentence. Scholars are almost in complete agreement that the order of the works is strictly that in which they were composed. The final phrase, "there are several other smaller works," has appeared to justify many students of the Isidorian tradition in continuously adding many other titles, but such attempts have usually been unsuccessful.[16] The notice that the writer himself (Braulio) has been responsible for dividing the *Etymologies* into books fits in exactly with statements in Braulio's letters and enables one to explain several statements in the correspondence between Isidore and Braulio.

The text adopted for this translation is that printed by

---

15 Pp. 335-40, 356-60. The title is *Renotatio Isidori a Braulione Caesaraugustano episcopo edita.*

16 See the new evaluation of the biographical and bibliographical accounts of Isidore in A. C. Vega, "Cuestiones críticas de las biografías Isidorianas," *Isidoriana: Estudios sobre san Isidoro de Sevilla en el XIV centenario de su nacimiento* (León 1961) 75-98, esp. 76-87 on Braulio. For Vega, who has studied the three oldest manuscripts (two titled *Renotatio* and one without title), Braulio's work has complete documentary and historical value: any work not mentioned there was not written by Isidore.

Galindo from the León manuscript, with certain modifica-
tions mentioned in the notes.[17] There is a partial English
translation with commentary in Brehaut[18] and a partial
French translation with commentary in Séjourné.[19] It should
be pointed out that the quotation from Cicero, of which
Lynch makes so much on pp. 218-219, is also found in
St. Augustine's *City of God* 6.2, and that Braulio almost
certainly took it from the latter rather than direct, as
we know from his *Letters* that he owned a copy of this famous
work by Augustine. In fact, every quotation of a classical
author found in Braulio almost certainly came to his knowledge in some Christian writer like Jerome or Augustine.

---

17 The most accessible text will be found in **PL** 81.15-17, also in **PL**
   82.65-68, both taken from Arévalo's edition of the works of Isidore
   (Rome 1797-1803).
18 Pp. 23-25.
19 Pp. 41-47.

BIBLIOGRAPHY

Brehaut, E. *An Encyclopedist of the Dark Ages: Isidore of Seville* (New York 1912).

Florez, H. and M. Risco. *España Sagrada* 30 (Madrid 1775).

Lynch, C. H. *Saint Braulio, Bishop of Saragossa (631-651): His Life and Writings* (Catholic University of America, Studies in Medieval History, N.S. 2; Washington 1938).

Lynch, C. H. and P. Galindo. *San Braulio, Obispo de Zaragoza (631-651), Su Vida y sus Obras* (Madrid 1950).

Madoz, J. *Epistolario de S. Braulio de Zaragoza* (Madrid 1941).

————. "Fuentes jeronimianas en el epistolario de S. Braulio de Zaragoza," *Gregorianum* 20 (1939) 407-22.

Migne, J. P. *Patrologiae Latinae Cursus Completus* (Paris 1844-1864) 80, 81, 82 (= PL)

Minguella de la Merced, T. *San Millán de la Cogolla: Estudos histórico-religiosos acerca de la patria, estado y vida de San Millán* (Madrid 1883).

Prudencio de Sandoval, M. F. *Primera parte de las fundaciones de los monesterios de S. Benito* (Madrid 1601).

Séjourné, P. *Le dernier père de l'Église: Saint Isidore de Séville* (Paris 1929).

Vasquez de Parga, L. S. *Braulionis Caesaraugustani Episcopi Vita S. Emiliani* (Madrid 1943).

11

LETTERS OF BRAULIO

LETTER 1

Isidore to the archdeacon Braulio, dearest and most beloved brother in Christ.[1]

Since I am not able to enjoy you with the eyes of the flesh, let me at least enjoy conversing with you, that I may be consoled by learning from a letter of yours of the good health of one whom I wish to see. It would be good if both were possible; but I may at least refresh myself concerning you mentally if I cannot do so bodily.

While we were together, I asked you to send me the sixth decade of St. Augustine.[2] Please find some way to make me acquainted with that work. I have sent you my little book called *Synonyms*,[3] not because it has any value, but because you wanted it. I commend to you this boy,[4] and I commend myself, that you may pray for wretched me, for I am much weighed down, both by the ills of the flesh and by the faults of my mind. For both I ask your aid, since I deserve nothing of myself.

Finally, I ask that, if I live long enough, you cause me to rejoice in hearing from you while there is a chance for the letter carrier to return to us.

---

1 Written 610-620.
2 *Commentaries on Psalms* 51-60.
3 A work on grammar.
4 Who carried the letter.

15

LETTER 2

Isidore to the archdeacon Braulio, most beloved son in Christ the Lord.[1]

When you receive a letter from your friend, dearest son, you would not hesitate to embrace it in place of your friend. When friends are separated, the second best consolation, if the beloved one is not present, is that his letter should be embraced in his stead.

I have sent you a ring because of my affection, and a pallium as the cloak of our friendship, which is the ancient source of this word.[2] Therefore, pray for me. May the Lord so fill you with grace that I may yet deserve to see you in this life, and that you will again delight with your presence one whom you saddened by your departure. I have sent you a small pamphlet of *Rules*[3] by my messenger Maurentio, the *primiclerius.*[4] Finally, I hope always to hear that you continue to be well, my beloved master and dearest son.

LETTER 3

Braulio, unworthy servant of the saints of God, to my lord and true lord and elect of Christ, Isidore, greatest of bishops.[1]

O pious lord and most excellent of men, I have been late in sending this request and slow in finding an opportunity

---

1 Written 610-620, perhaps earlier than *Letter* 1 and the earliest of the whole collection. It is first in the manuscript.
2 In the true Isidorian style, the author here assumes an etymological relation between *amictus* and *amicitia.*
3 This *quaternio* could have contained selected chapters from Isidore's *Regula monachorum,* which we still possess, or similar material.
4 He apparently had the task of distributing altar bread to clerics according to rank. This seems to be a different word from *primicerius,* the only form which is in the dictionaries. Cf. Madoz 74 n. 13.

---

1 Written in 625.

to write, because as my sins pile up I have been prevented from making my demands by a terrible invasion—not only by the evil of famine and poverty, but also by that of pestilence and the presence of the enemy.[2] Now, however, although oppressed by a thousand adversities and a thousand cares, after a long period of misery, as though aroused from the sloth of a shameful sleep, so to speak, I dare add a dutiful greeting to the words of my petition and, prostrate with humility of both heart and body, I beseech you to use the preeminent influence of your blessedness to keep commended ever to the end your special servant, whom you have always received with pious consideration and holy favor. For, so is Christ my witness, I am tortured with severe pain in that, after the passage of such a long time, I do not even yet deserve to see you face to face, but I hope in Him who does not forget to have tenderness,[3] and casts not off forever,[4] that He will hear the prayer of the poor[5] and restore me, though unworthy, to your presence.

I bring it to your attention and use every means of supplication to request that you be mindful of your promise and cause to be sent to your servant the book of *Etymologies,* which I hear is recently completed with the favor of God, for, as I am aware, a great part of your labor therein was performed at the insistence of your servant.[6] Be generous, first of all, with me, and so may you be blessed and first in the gatherings of the saints.

I ask you to use your influence with your son and lord, the king, to have sent to me right away the minutes of the council in which Sintharius was thoroughly cooked, even if

2 Madoz suggests that this may refer to the Vascones who invaded Tarragona in 621-624 and were successfully opposed by King Swinthila, as described by Isidore in *Historia Gothorum* era DCLIX n. 62-63 (ed. Mommsen MGH, *auct. ant.* 11.292-93 [Berlin 1894]).

3 Cf. Isa. 49.15.

4 Cf. Ps. 43.24.

5 Cf. Ps. 68.34.

6 For the relations suggested here between Isidore and Braulio, cf. the full discussion in Lynch, *op. cit.* 33-54.

not completely purified, with the fire of your inquisition.[7] I have already asked his highness for this, since I am very much in need of it to investigate the truth in the council.

Finally, I beseech the piety of the almighty Creator that, for the integrity of the faith and the stability of His Church, He preserve for a long time the crown of your blessedness, and that because of your intercession the most holy Trinity may fortify me against the dangers and countless difficulties of the present world and may restore me by your prayers to the bosom of your memory, safe from every tempest of sin.

And with his own hand.[8] I, Braulio, servant of the Lord, to Isidore: May I enjoy you in the Lord, O burning and never-failing light.[9]

LETTER 4

Isidore to Bishop Braulio, my lord and servant of God.[1]

I thank Christ that I have learned that you are well; would that I might see in the flesh the evidence of this health of which I have learned. I will tell you what befell me for my sins, since I was not worthy to read through your praise of me. At the very moment I received your note,[2] the king's slave came to me. I gave my attendant the note and immediately went to the king, intending to read it through later and answer it. When I got back from the palace, I not only did

---

7 Madoz suggests that the reference is to a possible synod held in Seville in 624 by the intervention of Isidore, in which a bishop, Sintharius, was presented for heretical views. No record of such a gathering is found in the surviving conciliar collections.

8 All the letters in this collection appear to have been dictated, but certain instructions show that the sender occasionally took the pen himself to add at the end an affectionate greeting or request to be remembered in prayer.

9 Cf. John 5.35.

---

1 Written in 632, probably in Toledo.

2 The Latin word is *pittacium*, described in Isidore's *Glossary* as "a short modest letter."

not find your writing, but everything else that was among
my papers had disappeared. For that reason, the Lord
knows, I wept for my lack of merit, for not having read your
letter. Please write to me again, whatever the occasion may be,
and do not take away the kindness of a word from yourself,
that what I have lost for my sins I may again receive by
your grace.

And with his own hand. Pray for us, blessed master.
Explicit.

LETTER 5

*Braulio, unworthy servant of the saints of God, to my lord
and true lord and elect of Christ, Isidore, greatest of bishops.*[1]

The interior spiritual man is usually filled with joy when
he experiences the inquisition of a friend. Hence, my
desire is, most reverent lord, if my faults do not present a
barrier, that you embrace my inquisition with kindness and
patiently receive criticism. For I shall deliver both: I am
performing the functions of an inquisition and I am directing
to you the reasons for my case against you. At the very
beginning and entrance of my discourse, prostrate before your
high apostolic dignity, I ask that you listen most kindly to
my petition. Although the presentation of criticism is weak-
ened by the interjection of tears, since tears are not signs of
criticism, still I hope that this criticism is tearful and these
tears critical; in either case, it is due to the license and presumption of love, not to the temerity of arrogance.

Now I shall present the introduction of my case. The
times are circling now to the seventh year, if I am not mistaken, since I recall having asked you for the books of
Origins[2] which you had composed. By various and diverse
methods, you cheated me when I was with you, and when I

---

1 Written in 632, not long after *Letter* 4, seven years after *Letter* 3.
2 Isidore called the work both *Etymologies* and *Origins*.

was absent, you answered absolutely nothing; but by subtle postponement, you either said the books were not finished yet, or they were not copied yet, or you had lost my letter, or many other excuses, until we have arrived at the present time and still without the accomplishment of my request. So I am going to turn my entreaties into complaints, to try to obtain by criticism and provocation what I could not by supplication. A beggar is often aided by loud use of his voice. Therefore, why, pray, my lord, do you not offer what you are asked for? Be sure of one thing: I shall not give up, pretending I did not want what I could not have, but I shall ask and I shall ask insistently, until I either receive it or drag it out of you, in the words of our most pious Redeemer, who bade: "Seek, and you shall find," and added: "Knock, and it shall be opened to you."[3] I have sought and I am asking, I am even knocking: I demand that you open. I am consoled by the discovery of this argument: that you will perhaps listen to the criticism of one whose requests you scorned. From, now on, I shall return your own methods, and you will recognize them; nor by foolish boasting do I presume to be so insipid as to put forth a new idea to one who is perfect. For I do not blush to speak to one who is most eloquent, inexperienced though I am, for I am mindful of the apostolic precept in which you are bidden "gladly to put up with the fool."[4]

Therefore, listen to the loud claims of my criticism. Why, I ask, do you still refuse the distribution of talents[5] and the dispensation of food[6] that have been entrusted to you? Now open your hand and grant a boon to your servants, lest they perish from want and hunger. You are aware what your creditor comes to ask of you. Whatever you give us will not be lessened for yourself. Recall that the multitude was satisfied with small loaves and that what was

---

3 Matt. 7.7.
4 Cf. 2 Cor. 11.19.
5 Cf. Matt. 25.15.
6 Cf. Gen. 47.12.

left over was greater than the amount of loaves.[7] Or do you
think that a gift bestowed on you is given solely for you?
It is both yours and ours; it is common, not private. Who
should be so foolish as to say that you should enjoy in private
what you know you enjoy to such an extent in common and
without sin? Since God has given you the management of his
treasures of wealth, safety, wisdom, and knowledge,[8] why do
you not generously pour out what you cannot lessen
by giving? Are you perhaps stingy with us because you find
nothing which you can get from us in exchange, although in
the members of His heavenly Body each one so possesses in
the other what he has not received in himself that he knows
that what he has should be possessed by the other? If you
give to one who has, you reap the fruit of such a small service.
But if you give to one who does not have, you satisfy the
Gospel precepts, so that it shall be restored to you at the
retribution of the just.[9] Accordingly, I am stricken with
remorse because I know of no good within myself to be
shared, since we are ordered "to serve one another in charity,"[10]
and each one to administer to another the grace which he has
received, "as good stewards of the manifold grace of God."[11]
"According as God has apportioned to each one the measure
of faith"[12] in one bond of members, each one should share
with the other parts, for "all these things are the work of one
and the same Spirit, who divides to everyone according as he
will."[13]

But now I return to the special resource which I promised to
use—persistent pleading, which is a friend to those in need of
friendship and which is not disguised with the grace of out-
ward decorations. So listen to my voice across so many inter-

---

7 Cf. Matt. 14.20.
8 Cf. Col. 2.3.
9 Cf. Luke 6.30-38.
10 Cf. Gal. 5.13.
11 1 Peter 4.10.
12 Rom. 12.3.
13 1 Cor. 12.11.

vening lands:[14] "Pay, pay what thou owest."[15] For you are a
servant, a servant of Christ and of Christians. Therein you
are greater than all of us, and the grace which you realize
was conferred upon you for our sake you should not
refuse to share with souls that are thirsty and tortured with
hunger for knowledge. Am I not the foot, which can nourish
the Church, the judge of the members, by running to obey the
commands of the belly and by showing obedience, and can I
not by following orders satisfy the demands of the sovereignty
of the head? Even though I know I am one of the less honorable members, let it suffice, for what you have clearly received
from the head, you may carry out through me; nor is it
proper for you not to heed me, for however unimportant, I
am redeemed by the Blood of Christ. "The head does not say
to the feet: 'I have no need of you.' Nay, much rather, those
that seem the more feeble members of the body are more
necessary; and those that we think the less honorable members
of the body, we surround with more abundant honor, and our
uncomely parts receive a more abundant comeliness."[16] Our
Creator and Dispenser so orders all things that love is increased when the divine gifts which one does not see in himself are bestowed to be possessed by another. Thus, then, the
manifold grace is well dispensed[17] when the gift received is
believed to belong also to him who does not have it, when it
is believed to have been given for the sake of him with whom
it is shared. The wisdom of your holiness knows very well that
this chapter of the apostle, already anticipated by us in part,[18]
applies entirely to this matter, and beyond doubt nothing
of what I have touched on here and there is unknown to you.
So it only remains, and this I most earnestly beseech, that you
fulfill these requests, not for my sake perhaps, but at least for

---

14 Jerome, *Ep.* 50.5 (CSEL 54.394); cf. notes to *Letter* 11.
15 Matt. 18.28.
16 1 Cor. 12.21-23.
17 Cf. 1 Peter 4.10.
18 1 Cor. 12.

the love divinely imparted, for which we are bidden to know and to bestow all things,[19] and without which all things are nothing. If any of my words, or rather my effusive language, is superfluous; if any of it is negligent; if any of it is useless or delivered without humility, I beg you to receive it all with kindness, to pardon everything, and to ask God to pardon everything.

Now, I have become aware that the books of the *Etymologies,* which I am requesting, my lord, are already in the hands of many others, though much mutilated and worn. So I am asking you to see fit to send me a copy that is written in full and corrected and carefully assembled, lest I become lost in envy and be forced to take vices for virtues from others. Although you are not in need of anything and although un-asked-for gifts have no value,[20] still I hope that your worthy grace will command something that we are willing and able to perform, so that you may partake of our services or, still better, may enjoy that love which is God.[21]

When these requests have been fulfilled, I shall have[22] some questions about the pages of Sacred Scripture, which may be answered for me by the light of your heart, if you do but command that light to shine upon us and to reveal the secrets of divine law. Even if I learn the answers which I am seeking, I shall not keep silent about the other matters; you open the way to winning confidence when, in the very beginning, you do not pierce me with the goads of shame, but grant occasion for pardon of my ignorance and, because you love me, however little I deserve it, you do not chide me; for it is a base and shameless thing to draw away from a friend before he is sated with your love.

As due to the homage that my lowly state entails, I add

---

19 Cf. 1 Cor. 13.1-3.
20 "Ultroneae putere mercedes" is a proverb found at least three times in Jerome's *Letters,* from which Braulio's use undoubtedly derives.
21 Cf. 1 John 4.16.
22 Reading *erunt* (Risco) for *erant* (Madoz).

the claims of my salvation, and I beg the piety of your most sacred mightiness to be pleased to pray for me, that by your intercession you may win a soul which is daily swamped with ills and may bring it to the gate of eternal rest, purified from its wretched, sinful state. It has been pleasant for me to speak at such length to you, as though I were in your presence and watching your every expression of emotion. That is why I did not hesitate to ramble on, though I may have incurred the charge of temerity. But I had to do one or the other to make you grant to my hasty, unjust manner what you refused to my humility. That is how bold I have become through the grace of your generosity. Therefore, if there be any cause for displeasure, that generosity can only blame itself that it loves so strongly as to remove fear, for "perfect love casts out fear."[23]

Relying for an exceptional favor upon an exceptional lord, in whom the strength of the holy Church abides, I suggest that, since our metropolitan Eusebius has died,[24] you give kind attention to the matter and mention it to your son, our lord,[25] that he should choose for that position one whose learning and holy ways may be an example to others. I commend this son in all ways to your most blessed highness, and both for the matters which I am requesting here, as well as for those which we have previously asked, may we deserve to be mentioned to him by you in a complimentary manner.

---

23 1 John 4.18.
24 Archbishop of Tarragona, 610-632.
25 King Sisenand, who, by this period, has assumed the right of intervention in church affairs, especially in the promotion of bishops.

LETTER 6

Isidore to my lord and servant of God, Bishop Braulio.[1]

The letters from your holiness reached me in the city of
Toledo, for although the command of the king had advised
me to turn back when I was already on the journey, I decided
not to interrupt my trip, because I was closer to seeing him
than to returning. I came into the king's presence; I found
there your deacon;[2] through him, I received and embraced
and read your words and thanked God for your safety, desir-
ing with all desire,[3] although ill and weak, to have the good
fortune in Christ of seeing you in this life, and confident of it,
for "hope does not disappoint, because of the charity which
is poured forth in our hearts."[4]

While still on the way, I sent you, among other manuscripts,
a manuscript of the *Etymologies,* and although it is uncor-
rected because of my poor health, I was intending to send it to
you to be emended as soon as I arrived at the site of the council. As for the appointment of a bishop of Tarragona, the
king's intention, so I learned, does not fall in with your
request, but he is not yet certain upon whom he will definitely
settle.[5] I request that you see fit to intercede with the Lord
for my sins, that by your prayer my faults may be remitted
and my crimes forgiven. *Likewise, with his own hand.* Pray
for us, most blessed lord and brother.

---

1 Written at Toledo late in 632 or early in 633. The Fourth Council
of Toledo, here postponed at the request of the king, actually convened on Dec. 5, 633.

2 Possibly Eugenius II, later metropolitan of Toledo; cf. below, *Letters*
31-33.

3 Cf. Luke 22.15.

4 Cf. Rom. 5.5.

5 The person finally chosen was Audax, who signed the minutes of the
Council in Dec., 633. Since the reference in *Letter* 5, last paragraph,
is a generalization with which the king could hardly disagree, Dom A.
Lambert (*Dict. d'hist. et de géog. eccl.* 5 [Paris 1931] 297, s.v. Audax)
proposed that there was a letter, not now preserved, from Braulio
to King Sisenand, which made a specific suggestion for the man to
be chosen.

LETTER 7

[At this point in the collection, Risco printed the very brief dedication found in many manuscripts of the *Etymologies*. It is now conceded that this dedication accompanied the first edition of the work, when it was presented to King Sisebut in 620. The manuscript of Braulio's *Letters* does not contain this letter, which was correctly bracketed by Madoz.]

LETTER 8

Isidore to my lord and servant of God, Bishop Braulio.[1]

With all desire have I desired[2] now to see your face; I pray that God may sometime grant this request before I die. For the present, however, please commend me to God in your prayers, that He may fulfill my hope in this life and may grant me to be associated with your blessedness in the future life. *And with his own hand.* Pray for us, most blessed lord and brother.

LETTER 9

Braulio to my lord Iactatus, the priest.[1]

I am informed, dearest brother, that you wish to demand from me some refreshment from the divine word, which I know to be beyond my power. I admire your devotion all the more in that you do not cease to demand the means of increasing your practice in divine studies, even when you have

---

1 Written a year or two before Isidore's death in 636.
2 Cf. Luke 22.15.

---

1 Written about 631-632. Iactatus is unknown except for *Letters* 9 and 10 to him, but he must have resided in western Spain, since it was natural for him to visit Tarazona, sixty miles west of Saragossa. An earlier letter from Iactatus is not preserved.

the knowledge that your questions cannot be answered. For since you meditate daily on the law of the Lord[2] and unfold the pages of the most blessed fathers and of most learned men, what can you find in us and how little can it be that you either wish to add to your own knowledge or concerning which you happen to foster a holy desire? It is enough and more than enough to read your friend, St. Augustine, also Jerome and Hilary and other most learned men, whom it would take me too long to mention by name and with whom you are certainly well acquainted. Let their words feed you, their thoughts instruct you; in fact, they can teach you completely all that you ask, and if you are satisfied with them, you need not bring out into the open our humble poverty,[3] nor expose us naked and visible to the eyes of the envious.

One matter important to me—even though I cannot actually realize it, still I want it to come true—is to ask the singular and inexhaustible piety of our common Lord and Redeemer to bestow upon you and upon us a life of happiness in common association and to grant us an opportunity of visiting, so that we may speak face to face and feed on mutual conversation and enjoy the peace in the Lord that we anticipate.

I also ask you to pray for me, in order that this may be brought to pass as quickly as I desire; I think it can easily be realized, if your holiness will come to us when you are visiting Tarazona.

As for the relics of the most revered apostles, which you have asked me to send, I truthfully reply that I have not a single martyr's relics so preserved that I can know whose they are. My lords and predecessors were of the opinion that the labels should be removed from all of them to make them indistinguishable, and that they should all be put in a single

---

2 Cf. Ps. 1.2.
3 Note the remarkable assonance in the Latin: "eis contentus nostram paupertatulam nec in propatulo trahas." *Paupertatula* is an unusual diminutive found in both Jerome and Augustine.

room, since, in many ways, either by theft or against their wills or by the coercion of the piety of many, they were being forced either to give away or to lose what they had. Some seventy were set apart, however, and are in common use, but among them are to be found none of those which you requested.

Finally, it is in place to greet you warmly, and most insistently, again and again, to ask you to pray for us. I have dictated hurriedly, just as my thoughts came to me; if I have overlooked anything, consider that it was not intentional.

LETTER 10

To the most holy priest Iactatus, venerable brother in Christ.[1]

While I was buried and completely distracted by cares, your letter brought me back to myself. With our attention absorbed as it is in the cares of the world and in the storms and tempests which daily threaten shipwreck for us in our present situation,[2] we are not allowed to be what we are said to be or what we should be. But when your letter gave me inspiration, I put everything behind me, and contemplated only you and me, putting nothing else between us except that love which is the Creator of both. Turning to Him and longing to thank Him, I could find nothing worthy of Him; I only recall that I tried; for such an insignificant creature cannot say thanks for such a great gift. Hence, if the thanks due to Him are inexpressible, I turn them over to you in the hope that they might fulfill my duties of recompense and devotion.

For I confess that I feel myself bound by those very same most unusual restrictions of which you complained, and I ask

---

1 Written about 631-632, some time after *Letter* 9.
2 A possible reference to the revolts which Sisenand had to quell after 631, before he consolidated his position as king.

myself why those who share one love should have to be
separated at such a distance, and why they should have companions with whom they do not wish to associate, and why
they should lack those whom they want to have. Once again
I am aware that this is not the home of the pious and that
they are separated in the regions of mortals in order that they
may be joined in the land of the living. It should be enough
for pilgrims to keep unbroken the ties of love, and thus to be
consoled in Him and constantly devoted to the law of Him
who truly is love,[3] even though they be separated from their
dear ones in the flesh, that the love that sweetens the memory
of absent ones may be itself sweet when dear ones are apart.
But if you truly loved me, you would do away with all delays,
you would hasten to start, you would come to me, and no distance, no occasion of any interference would stand in the way.
No, start up as if with spurs, pierce your mind with goads, and
arouse the force of your love and the fire of your affection to
such a point that it may burst into flames that cannot be
quenched with deep water.[4] Why have I said all this? Because
you visited Tarazona, where you very often stay, and would
not come to see me. Confess your guilt if you wish to be
pardoned, and seek diligently to make it possible for yourself
to appear to us directly after Easter.

I salute you in the Lord Jesus Christ with abundant and
manifold affection, asking in many ways and earnestly that
you commend me to my Creator most promptly in your
prayers; may the omnipotence of Christ the Lord increase
within you, and perfect its increase, and preserve its perfected
grace.

You have sent us what is offered in the sacrament of the
Body of Christ; we have sent you what prefigures the Blood
in the mystery of the same Lord, namely, two measures of
wine. We have also sent a measure of oil and a measure of

---

3 Cf. 1 John 4.8.
4 Cf. Cant. 8.7.

olives in accordance with the double precept of charity: that is to say, one by which the love of God is signified, and the other, love of neighbor. We have sent one measure[5] of damson plums, about which I cannot find anything symbolic to say, unless, perchance, it is that, when the Lord was born, the special attribute of that city from which this kind of fruit comes[6] was sent as an offering: this is the gold which the Holy Gospel mentions as given by the Magi.[7]

LETTER 11

Braulio to my lord, the priest Tajo.[1]

Your thoughts are so agitated and you are so tossed by the stormy blasts of impatience that it is fair to say: "O thou of little patience, why art thou disturbed?"[2] I wish you were equally moved to take refuge in humility, rather than to turn to abuse and harsh words. For you may be quite sure, I say it with God as my witness, that, when I wrote about that donkey in my letter and told you to climb onto it, I was joking and not intending to censure you, which should be easy to understand from my facetious tone. You, on the contrary, became indignant, like Aesop's jackdaw,[3] and told me to

---

5 The liquid measure is *metrum,* the dry measure *modius.*
6 Damascus.
7 Cf. Matt. 2.11.

---

1 Braulio had written to Tajo, his future successor in the see of Saragossa, humorously chiding him for lack of humility, and trying to repress his youthful hotheadedness, including a phrase equivalent to "Go, climb on a donkey"; Tajo, very indignantly and with no sense of humor, had replied: "Go, climb on a camel," referring doubtless to a Visigothic custom of humbling rebellious nobles by making them ride in a team drawn by camels.
2 Cf. Matt. 14.31.
3 Phaedrus, *Fabulae* 1.3, has Aesop give an example of a jackdaw which decked itself out with peacock's feathers. The words in the manuscript are *gragulus Isopius* and Braulio probably borrowed the material through some other intermediary not yet identified, or it may have

go climb on a camel and to watch out not to bang my head
on the church doors. This you poured out without much elegance, with less wisdom, and more evil purpose than on previous occasions, not realizing that our Head, which is Christ,[4]
does not hurl Himself against the doors of the church, though
He may against "the synagogue of Satan."[5] The shame herein
seems to us to lie not in the words but in the sentiment; we
do not at all blame your ignorance, but we wish your attitude
were more humble, for it is patient endurance of criticism
which shows a man's humility, and how much of that you have
can be learned in the present situation.

What can I say about the rest of what you wrote? Trying
to clear yourself of the charges, you only make the charges
appear more sordid; if I wanted to answer them, and they
certainly deserve censure, it would not be difficult at all nor
would it require much effort, since all it would take to destroy
your objections would be to oppose them with counter-
propositions of the same topics. But not to let my story cause
a long delay,[6] I have master Leo as witness of my intentions,
and actually you yourself, for though ungrateful and unwilling, while you were saying you were hurt by my words, you
also admitted that they had definite bearing on your moral
progress.

Briefly, not to offend a friend by speaking too long, I want
you to know that I can bite back if I wish, that when I am
hurt, I can inflict a real wound.[7] For I, too, with Flaccus,
"have learned my letters and often drawn my hand away
from the ruler";[8] of us it can be said: "He has hay in his
horns, flee far away";[9] or still better, these words of Vergil:

---

been a common proverb. *Gragulum Aesopi* is found in Tertullian,
Against the Valentinians 12 (CSEL 47.191).

4 Cf. 1 Cor. 11.3.

5 Apoc. 2.9.

6 Cf. Ovid, *Fasti* 2.248.

7 Cf. Persius, *Satires* 1.115.

8 Really Juvenal, *Satires* 1.15.

9 Horace, *Satires* 1.4.34.

"We too, father, with our right hands hurl weapons and an
iron that is not weak; the wounds we inflict also draw blood."[10]

For that model exercise of yours, composed in a contest, how
trite it was to me and, as they say, trampled underfoot, except for that part which, asking pardon of Gregory,[11] I
noticed was pilfered or rather spoiled. In our anxiety to
preserve love and not to lose you, we overlook all of this
and do not put in anything which might cause laughter, lest
our story arouse ungrateful mirth, as Ovid[12] says, and lest, as
Appius says, we seem to be practicing canine eloquence.[13] But
as I have said, putting all this aside, we carry out the duties
of our own office and preserve the humility of our Master the
Lord Christ, preferring to follow Him who said: "I gave my
back to the lashes and my cheeks to palms;"[14] "who, when he
was reviled, did not revile, when he suffered, did not threat-
en."[15] Therefore, let us, too, dearest friend, spurn the former
examples and follow these more pleasant ones; let us cast off
the bitterness that comes through various suspicions. For the
Lord knows that I had not the slightest intention of suggesting
some of the things that you wrote in your letter, and I did not

---

10 Vergil, *Aeneid* 12.50-51. This entire paragraph, except for the first
phrase, was discovered by Madoz in Jerome's *Letter* 50.5. The invective
is Jerome's, adapted by Braulio. The words "with Flaccus" and "these
words of Vergil" are not in Jerome. I suggest that they had been
inserted in the margin of Braulio's copy of Jerome's *Letters*, and that
he wrongly included the Flaccan identification with the quotation
from Juvenal. The two biblical quotations in the next paragraph
are from the same passage in Jerome. The supposed classical learning
of Braulio is less direct than it was once taken to be. There is no
evidence that he read Ovid, Horace, Vergil, Persius, and Juvenal at
first hand.

11 The works of Gregory the Great had begun to be known in Spain
and Braulio had read them, although he does not quote from them.
The Latin of this sentence is forced and obscure. "In a contest" is my
translation of *in armatura*, for which Galindo reads "de tanto
aparato."

12 Cf. Ovid, *Fasti* 3.738.

13 Jerome, *Letter* 134.1 (CSEL 56.261) has these words attributed to
Appius.

14 Cf. Isa. 50.6.

15 1 Peter 2.23.

dictate them in the sense in which you understood them; in other matters, too, I see you did not clearly appreciate what I said, if you will forgive me for saying so, for your answers did not agree with what I wrote. Because wrong or suspicion has been thrown between us by some enemy, let us both reject him and let us abide in Christ and in the unanimity of our love; this is what I increasingly hope.

But if it pleases my God, I will go there and I think I shall quickly obtain pardon from you for those words which I wrote exactly as I meant them. Meanwhile, you have refused my affection to such an extent that, in your indignation, you attribute the result to your own petition. Not only am I unmoved by your mistaken accusations, but I received your letter calmly, and if I have offended you, I ask your pardon and beg you to love me more and more, mindful that we are Christians and must fear rather than pursue the loss of our souls.

Now, if you have been upset before, it is time to put an end to it. One who is more fond of wine than of words must be careful that wine does not make his words bring harm to him. Look, while I was striving to make a pitcher, as Terence said, my hands produced a jar.[16] For I had intended to write just a short note, but I have produced a rather prolix letter; but you have written a testament instead of a letter, such as may perhaps not be confirmed until after your death, since it cannot legally be unsealed now.[17]

Goodbye, my dearest friend, deserving to be loved by me with all love, and forgive me that, in presuming too much of your fondness, I even write to you at too great length.

---

16 Really Horace, *Art of Poetry* 21-22. Braulio probably found the quotation in Jerome, *Letter* 107.3, where there is no ascription. I think he gave it to Terence because of a marginal note in his manuscript of Jerome. He uses the same words in *Letters* 36 and 44, and much later Tajo himself used them in a letter to Eugenius II. Since these were both pupils of Braulio, it must have been a well-known phrase in their circle. Only this once, however, is the name of Terence given as author.

17 Cf. Heb. 9.16, 17.

LETTER 12

Braulio, unworthy servant of the saints of God, to my lord Floridius, archdeacon.[1]

I faithfully confess, dear son, that when I received your letter, I was in the midst of such anxious cares and distracting concerns that, although I was glad to hear that you were well, I could not send an early answer to your requests for fear that I might "in hasty discussion pour out what you sought, not in the hurried manner of a writer but with the rashness of dictation," or that I might not completely explain everything necessary concerning these matters, which if not discussed as fully as seems proper, "become a cause for downfall rather than a source of knowledge."[2] "For a most difficult time is at hand, when it seems to me much better to be silent than to speak, so that the zeal of the zealous may cease," all the more so of the slothful, since it is proper for us to think on the necessity of salvation and the brevity of life rather than "with Appius, to use canine eloquence."[3]

And so, although you have asked me to send something suited to your thought, still, since the time found me hindered by various circumstances, as I have already said, it was better to ask your pardon than not to satisfy you fully. Therefore, asking your pardon, I request you to pour forth your prayers for me before the Lord, that my sin may be forgiven through your intercession. Further, if God lets me see you, I shall explain face to face what you want better than I can write it while absent.

In short, unless one first knows something about those numbers in the Greek language, it will not be easy to understand this, for they have one meaning in Greek and another in Latin, and the prolixity of such a task requires almost

---

1 Written about 632. A Floridius was bishop of Segorbe in 647.
2 Jerome, *Letter* 112.1 (**CSEL** 55.367-68).
3 Jerome, *Letter* 134.1 (**CSEL** 56.261), as quoted in *Letter* 11 above.

the length of a book instead of a letter,[4] if everything is to be explained clearly and nothing is to be omitted. But, as I said, it is easier to explain person to person, "for the living voice has some sort of hidden vitality and sounds stronger when diffused in the ear,"[5] while the listener can make it known when he does not understand, and the instructor knows when he should slow down to explain more clearly. I should prefer, in view of the demands of time, as the apostle said: since "the time is short,"[6] to devote my efforts to "love which edifies," rather than to "knowledge, which it is difficult to keep from puffing up"[7] or being exposed to envy. But since I know you are so very anxious to use your knowledge, I shall humor you, and I shall compose this letter so as not to dismiss you uninstructed. Now it is your turn to approach the subject scientifically with your known acuteness and great intelligence, or to wait for me to send you an exposition.

Finally, I send you my most weighty greeting and most profuse requests that you refresh me with further words as soon as you have an opportunity.

LETTER 13

Braulio, unworthy servant of the saints of the Lord, to my master Fronimian, priest and abbot.[1]

When I learn that you are sad because of imminent trials, I, too, become equally sad, but what must be done in such a

---

4 Cf. Jerome, *Letter* 133.13 (CSEL 56.260).
5 Cf. Jerome, *Letter* 53.2 (CSEL 54.446).
6 1 Cor. 7.29.
7 Cf. 1 Cor. 8.1.

---

1 Written some time after *Letter* 14, to Fronimian, to dissuade him from his plan to give up his position as abbot. This Fronimian is, with fair probability, identified with Braulio's brother of the same name, to whom was addressed the *Life of St. Emilian*. Fronimian has been called by Dom Lambert abbot of the original monastery of San Millán; cf. "La famille de Saint Braulio et l'expansion de la Règle de Jean de Biclar," *Universidad* 10 (1933) 78.

MILLS COLLEGE
LIBRARY

situation can be determined by your own wisdom better than
by any suggestions I may be able to offer in discussing the
matter. You well know, my lord, that the monastic life has no
need of more penance, exposed as it is to daily humility and
spiritual trials, so that in all the events of life, it is constantly
associated with penance. But it is better to see that you do not,
for the sake of your own repose, lose the reward you have
earned over such a long period, lest you completely lose the
credit you have achieved in trying to increase your deserts.
It is serious for you to turn away from concern for the
brothers, or rather to have little regard for the fact that you
are in charge of those who are fond of you. Concerning what
has happened, I urge and beg you to take your time about
such actions, so that you will not incur disgrace and cause
to be upset that tranquillity which you have enjoyed so long.
Therefore, it is fitting that in what concerns this life of yours,
of which you will have to render account to God, you should
not give up your concern for the brothers and should not put
in charge of them an abbot whom they do not want, so that
you may avoid disgrace and enjoy during your life peace
and the reward of your learning and labor. Do not even consider what will happen later, when the Ruler of the universe
will govern that congregation according to His own dispensation.

For I confess, my lord, that I am not a little amazed that
you are so upset by all these scandalous events that arise
on every occasion that you wish to withdraw from the authority derived from your seniority and prefer to spend your
life in silence rather than to stay in the duties which
have been entrusted to you. Where will your blessed perseverance be if your patience fails? Be mindful of the apostle
who said: "Tribulation works out endurance";[2] also: "All
who want to live piously in Christ Jesus will suffer persecu-

---

2 Rom. 5.3.

tion."[3] Endurance exists not only in confessing the name of
Christian by sword and fire and various kinds of punishment,
but differences in customs, the insults of the disobedient and
the barbs of wicked tongues, and various temptations are included in this kind of persecution; there is not a single
occupation that is without its dangers. Who will guide the
ship among the waves if the pilot quits his post? Who will
guard against wolves if the shepherd does not watch?[4] Or who
will drive away the robber if sleep removes the watchman from
the sight of his outlook? You must stick by the work entrusted
to you and the task you have undertaken; you must observe
justice and show mercy; you must hate the sins, not the men;
you must strengthen the weak and correct the proud. Even
though tribulation brings us more than we can endure, let us
not be afraid as if we were resisting with our own strength;[5]
we must pray with the apostle that God give us "the way out
with the temptation,"[6] that we may be able to withstand, for
Christ is both our courage and our counsel, "without Him we
can do nothing,"[7] and "with Him we can do all things."[8]

Lo, I am become wordy in trying to answer your questions,
but to go back to what I said at the very beginning, you know
better yourself, my lord, that none should be placed in charge
of those who do not want him, lest they pay no attention to
him or hate him and become less devoted to religion in trying
to find occasion for strife. Those who receive one whom they
do not wish will not obey him as they should, and through
their inobedience, scandal arises and they lose their religious

---

3 2 Tim. 3.12.
4 Cf. John 10.12.
5 The entire paragraph to this point is borrowed directly from *Letter* 167
  of Leo the Great (PL 54.1200-01), praef. Leo was writing to Rusticus,
  Bishop of Narbo, who wanted to give up his episcopacy because of a
  quarrel with some priests, as Fronimian here desires to withdraw as
  abbot. Braulio has quoted extensively, though not always with verbal
  exactness, this remarkably apt passage.
6 Cf. 1 Cor. 10.13.
7 Cf. John 15.5.
8 Cf. Phil. 4.13.

intentions. It is the duty of your wisdom to temper all such acts, to display the sweetness of affection, and to place the future in the hope of God, for you should have the wisdom both to guide them and to preserve a quiet life for yourself; and they should be able, under your leadership, to serve God with utmost devotion. They cannot be obedient if they are goaded into being stubborn, and it will be a dreadful calamity if, in providing for the future, we upset the order of obedience in the present.

I have received everything that you sent me; for everything I have expressed thanks and still do not cease to do so. But I pray Christ the Lord that He may in His clemency preserve and adorn your life and the eminence of your blessedness in return for my aid and intercession before God, for I know that I am unequal to making sufficient reply to such services.

Meanwhile, please pray for me, your servant, for we, too, have our temptations and are affected with various ills. Hence, I beg you to support me by your prayers rather than grieve for me when I have been crushed by shipwreck.

LETTER 14

Braulio to my lord Fronimian, priest and abbot.[1]

We do not have enough parchment for ourselves and so I have none to send you; but I have sent you the price, with which you will be able to buy some if you order it. As for the *Commentary on the Apostle*[2] which we have sent you, first read it through carefully and put everything in order. Since the manuscript has the opinions of various authors written in the margin,[3] incorporate them in the text as you find them to

---

1 Written some time after Isidore's death (636), but probably a few years earlier than *Letter* 13, which it actually precedes in the manuscript.
2 Braulio does not state clearly whether he wrote this commentary on Paul himself or gathered the material from various sources.
3 Interpretation of *ad aurem* suggested by Madoz 106 n. 4.

be in agreement with the Catholic faith, and in the proper
order; then, copy them so carefully that the commentary will
follow through each chapter, rather than having the work
split up on separate pages as it is now; otherwise, we shall
write it over again after you send it.

After your fashion, my lord, you send to inquire from me
about matters which you know very well; in trying to display
your humility, you but show up our ignorance. If the answer
which I am about to give proves careless in any respect, look
to yourself for the cause, for you ask me to give more than
you gave and you try to get out of me more than you put in
while training me. You ask me whether on Good Friday after
each lesson the response should be an *Amen,* or whether,
in usual fashion, a *Gloria* should be chanted. Now, this is not
the custom with us, nor have I seen it done anywhere, nor was
it done by my lord Isidore of most blessed memory, not
even at Toledo nor at Gerona. In Rome, they say, no office
is celebrated that day. I suppose it is for no other reason
than that the memory of the Passion of our Lord may always
be renewed and the true sadness of our hearts in His Body
may be revealed by a sign of that season; or perhaps to signify
the perturbation of the apostles, who deserted their duty
on that day; or rather, perhaps, because the Church beginning
in Peter from that day started out in sorrow that it might
reap the joy in the Resurrection.

Or is it because every Christian living this life piously
in the likeness of Christ "must enter the kingdom of God
through many tribulations,"[4] and so this admonition of sorrow is signified to us in the renewed revolution of the year
in Christ, so that thus Christ may be imitated beyond doubt?
I think another reason for recalling the sorrow of that night[5]
is that the things which were performed visibly by Christ in
the flesh may be fulfilled by the Church, which is still visible

---

4 Cf. Acts 14.21.
5 On Holy Saturday.

in this world. For just as the Resurrection of the Lord, signified by Easter, is simple in joy, so ours is double, both in the present, that is, and in future time, and so it is necessary that on that day the sorrow represented by the form of our present life be set aside and the joy in the glorious Resurrection of our Redeemer be assumed in its place.

You see I have mentioned the various things that have occurred to me and as briefly as possible. You have the right to use your own judgment in selecting anything of which you approve and in correcting or deleting anything that has displeased you.

Concerning the covering of the altar and the veils to be used, the custom of the churches is that as evening approaches the church is decorated and the true light, arising from below, is received with pomp, because those virgins who kept their lamp trimmed awaited the arrival of the Bridegroom in the joy of the Resurrection.[6] Thus, the feast is celebrated during the night until midnight, at which hour we believe that we ourselves shall arise from the dead and that the Lord "will judge the living and the dead";[7] for what has already occurred in the Head will follow in the members.

Finally, I devotedly add the humble service of my servility, and entrust myself to your prayers, to be saved as I am tossed upon the storms of this life, if only God may look down from heaven and pardon me and pity those whom we so unworthily lead.

LETTER 15

Braulio, unworthy servant of the saints of God, to Basilla, my mistress and dearest daughter in Christ.[1]

Tossed by the storms of this terrible message, I am com-

---

6 Cf. Matt. 25.1-13.
7 2 Tim. 4.1.

---

1 Written about 633, to console his sister for the death of her husband.

pelled without being asked to answer your letter, and my mind does not know where to turn first: whether to declare my own sorrow or to offer you consolation; or, if it be not out of place, to mention my present good health, if a life afflicted with sorrows can be called good health. For lo, daily the good are leaving the Church and the bad are increasing daily, and we are saddened as much by the defection of the one as by the progress of the other. As a matter of fact, the apostle forbids us to mourn for our dead;[2] but who does not grieve when he loses a present good? For the "chosen vessel"[3] himself rejoices that Epaphras[4] was restored to him from the neighborhood of death, in which he must have had both joy over his own recovery and doubtless sorrow at his death. We are encouraged to hope when we do not doubt that the life of the faithful is exchanged for a better one, and we have them as stronger pleaders in the presence of God, by whose loss we are, for the time being, made destitute here. Yet somehow, amid the encouragement to consolation and the hope of resurrection, no matter how strongly the mind believes, it is crushed by a feeling of loss,[5] but since no other way of escape is offered, we must use all our strength to embrace this one, for in Him that "condones the wicked"[6] and "raises up the dead,"[7] "hope does not disappoint,"[8] because we believe that we shall be in that blessed region with those who already sleep.

"One who is overcome by his own grief" and who weeps and sobs so much that he cannot speak "is not the best one to offer consolation."[9] For lo, as I in my sadness try to console you in yours, "the tears run down my face,"[10] and, try as I will,

---

2 Cf. Jerome, *Letter* 3.3 (CSEL 54.15); also 1 Thess. 4.13.

3 Acts 9.15.

4 Phil. 2.25-28, where the reference is to Epaphroditus; there is also an Epaphras mentioned by Paul, e.g., Col. 1.7.

5 Jerome, *Letter* 60.2 (CSEL 54.550).

6 Prov. 17.15.

7 Cf. John 6.40.

8 Rom. 5.5.

9 Borrowed from Jerome, *Letter* 39.2 (CSEL 54.295).

10 Jerome, *Letter* 22.35 (CSEL 54.198).

I cannot hide my feelings. How can we help it when one and the same fate awaits each of us after the sin of our mortality? Pious and impious, just and wicked, moral and worthless are all carried off, but the saint and the damned shall not be joined by one judgment and one cohabitation in the hereafter. Therefore, let us endure the bitterness of the present life, patiently awaiting what we shall some day be, and let us rejoice in the Lord for our hope of a happy life, praying and beseeching that He will be completely appeased when He meets both our dear ones who have gone before and us who follow, and that He shall never separate us by His severe judgment; but rather that "mercy triumphs over judgment"[11] and with His accustomed piety, if it shall be agreeable to Him, He may unite us in the eternal blessedness of His storehouse.

Let us be animated with this hope, let us serve Him with this purpose, and let us find in Him both the affection of His love and the source of consolation. I urge and request you especially, my dear sister, to exhibit the measure of your consolation so prudently, both to yourself and to all who are grieved by the loss of such a husband, that you "may appear to be waiting for him rather than to have lost him,"[12] and do not grieve that you have lost such a protector, but rejoice that you had such a husband.[13]

Finally, I greet you all with equal affection, and I ask you all with equal supplication to pray for me and to bear with equanimity this sorrow that has befallen. I am not unaware of the degree of woe which this sad news has brought to you.

---

11 James 2.13.
12 Jerome, *Letter* 60.14 (CSEL 54.568).
13 Jerome, *Letter* 60.7 (CSEL 54.556).

LETTER 16

Braulio, unworthy servant of the saints of God, to Apicella, mistress and daughter in Christ.[1]

Although this book was written for another, I am sending it to you, because I did not want to refuse your request. In fact, I think it happened by the will of the Almighty that it should be given to you, although prepared for another. For you have herein holy Tobias, the loss of whose sight[2] may console you for the loss of your husband; and you have Judith, who, in the adornment[3] of her widowhood, may teach you to beautify your widowhood with virtues, and may show you the mortification in your body for which Holophernes set an example,[4] in order that you may attain the blessing of your race and of your faith and have the name and perpetual memory of blessed[5] in future posterity.

Farewell in the Lord, and please remember and pray for us.

LETTER 17

Braulio, unworthy servant of the saints of God, to Wiligildus, bishop and my lord in Christ, most blessed lord, to be venerated in the members of Christ and to be embraced with all love.[1]

I am not unaware that I acted contrary to the edicts of the fathers and the decrees of the canons when I raised to sub-

---

1 Written probably 633-634, accompanying the biblical texts of Tobias and Judith, to console the noblewoman Apicella for the death of her husband.
2 Cf. Tob. 2.11.
3 Cf. Judith 10.3.
4 Cf. Judith 13.10.
5 Cf. Judith 15.10.

---

1 Written probably in 633-634. The addressee appears to have had a see in Visigothic territory outside of Spain.

deacon and deacon a monk who, as I well know, ran away from a monastery under your control, for although the Church of Christ is diffused throughout the whole world, it is yet considered one in Catholic universality, since it relies upon its rectors and is governed by its prelates; it is both divided in privileges and one in the bond of faith; for this reason, I realize that I exceeded my authority. I have been the more anxious to set this at the very beginning of this letter that, having confessed my sin, I may more swiftly receive the indulgence of pardon. For I reflect that although the guidance of the churches is shared in many ways by a diversity of bishops, still I recall that it is one beyond a doubt and I am animated by the hope of charity, which has caused me to presume so much on your part and almost to destroy the correct authority, for charity, as one of the fathers said, knows no rank,[2] or with the apostle: "Charity is not self-seeking."[3] When I assumed your authority, I did not try to make it my own, but I believed you would do the same thing if I asked you to spare him. So I gave orders to your servant, but not without testimony and questioning about his manner of living. Therefore, although the great distance of land between us makes me immune to your authority, I ask you to pardon me as well as him, so that herein you may show your kindness, when you display your piety and goodness by forgiving me in his presence. If I obtain this, then, I ask you to permit him to keep the orders which he received from me, or rather accepted by my unworthy hands, and to supplicate Christ the Lord incessantly for my unworthiness, not only so that I may know that I have received pardon from you, but that also I may realize that I am supported with the help of your prayer, and in the mortality of this life am so manifestly aided by the Lord.

With religious humility and most devoted servitude, I pay

---

2 Cf. Jerome, *Letter* 7.6 (CSEL 54.31).
3 1 Cor. 13.5.

my respects to your beatitude and ask that, when you have
the occasion, I may merit being included among your corres-
pondents. The same for Ayulfus, priest and abbot.[4]

LETTER 18

*Braulio, unworthy servant of the saints of God, to my
mistress and daughter in Christ, Pomponia, abbess.*[1]

I am pierced by one wound and tortured with much grief,
the bond of bitterness does not permit the tongue to perform
its function, and it is easier to weep than to talk.[2] Lo, one
affliction comes upon another affliction, and contrition upon
contrition: "as if a man were to flee from a lion, and a bear
should meet him," or howl at being struck by a scorpion,
"and a snake should bite him";[3] so completely am I dejected
and afflicted with the misery of my sorrow. I confess, madam,
that every time I try to write to you about the passing of our
lady Basilla of blessed memory, I am overcome with bitterness
and experience a dullness in my mind, a heaviness in my
senses, and a slowness in my tongue, because, while I was occu-
pied with grief, my mind was affected by death. As time passed
and my grief was sufficiently lightened for me to express myself in words, I was again struck with redoubled woe and dis-
solved in tears. The terrible news was brought to me of the
death of Bishop Nunnitus,[4] my lord of blessed memory. Thus
depressed, I utter but few words and sobs. O what good we
have lost for our time in these two! What light of truth!

---

4 Ayulfus was probably abbot of the monastery from which the unknown
   monk had fled. There was an Aviulfus known to have been a bishop
   in Aquitania.

1 Written to his sister in 634 or 635 to lament the death of their other
   sister, Basilla (cf. *Letter* 15).
2 Gregory the Great, *Hom.* 33 on the Gospels, first sentence (PL 76.1239).
3 Amos 5.19.
4 Nunnitus, Bishop of Gerona, attended the council at Toledo in Dec.,
   633, but died before 636.

What an example of good deeds, what intercession for our sins! Where now is the protection before God that we enjoyed in them? Where is refuge for the wretched? Where is hospitality for pilgrims? Where is comfort and rest for monks and nuns? You must understand what I mean but am unable to express; I merely indicate my thoughts, for I cannot begin to say good of them, knowing that it would be a completely impossible task for me to try to catalog their most holy acts, even if I professed facility of words, grace of tongue, and ingenuity of memory. Still, as I said, I can show how much I grieve and how much grief I feel within me.

Woe, woe to this present life; how much better it is to bemoan it than to embrace it, to hate than to love! The good passes, the bad succeeds, and with constant course we pass by. It must be some drunken stupor of the mind that makes us think we shall endure, for insensibly time passes, the death to come approaches, and our hope presents us with images of present joys only. Happy are they whose joy is God and whose rejoicing is in the blessedness of the future, whose sufferings and disgrace are hidden with Christ in the standard of His Cross to be remembered at the eternal triumph! So let all our affection be directed towards Him, all our service displayed in Him, that our inner man may be consoled by Him who suffered for us; may He not abandon us anywhere or at any time.

Therefore, use the meditation of the Sacred Scriptures to console your spirit, and through you let the other sisters be consoled, and at the same time kindly pray that, with the aid of your prayer amidst the shipwrecks and the varied dangers of this life, the Divine Omnipotence may extend to me the comfort of His piety, that I may deserve with you to enjoy the presence of the Omnipotence in the future life.

I salute all who are bound with you to the servitude of Christ the Lord; above all I greet you with special piety and ask that you confer your holy love upon me, just as you have realized the love which is His gift to me. You do nothing unusual if you love me, for you know the nature of my heart and what a companion shares your blood. Explicit.

LETTER 19

Braulio to his honored daughters Hojo and Eutrocia.[1]

I know, I know that he who needs to be consoled does not offer the best consolation and that those who are overcome by their own sobs cannot well relieve another's grief,[2] but since the fall of man, this law has been given to the world and this is the sentence of God, that bitter death shall cut down all men whom birth has brought to light; both you and I must use this fact as a solace to remind ourselves that in the death of our friend Hugnan we are neither the first nor the last to experience this. That we may reflect upon better and loftier things, let us recall that Christ, the hope of all believers, calls those who have departed from the world sleeping, not dead,[3] saying: "Lazarus, our friend, sleeps."[4] But the holy apostle does not wish us to mourn for those who sleep.[5] Therefore, if our faith holds that all who believe in Christ according to the Holy Gospel shall not die forever,[6] we know by faith that he is not dead and that we shall not die. "For the Lord himself shall come down from heaven with cry of command, and with voice of archangel, and with trumpet of God; and the dead who are in him will rise."[7] Therefore, let the hope of resur-

---

1 Written about 635-638. Hugnan, just deceased, was son of Hojo and husband of Eutrocia, possibly also father of Hermenfred, mentioned at the end of the letter.
2 Cf. Jerome, *Letter* 39.2; cf. Braulio, *Letter* 15 n. 5.
3 Cf. Jerome *Letter* 60.2 (CSEL 54.550).
4 John 11.11.
5 Jerome, *Letter* 3.3 (CSEL 54.15) with probable reference to 1 Thess. 4.13-18.
6 Cf. John 11.26.
7 Cf. 1 Thess. 4.16.

rection inspire us that we shall again see there those whom
we lose here; we have only to believe well in Him and obey
His commandments, with whom is all power, that He can
more easily arouse the dead than we those who sleep.[8]

In spite of these words, we are so deeply affected that we
fall into tears and the longing of desire crushes the beliefs
of the mind. How miserable is man's lot! How vain is all our
life without Christ! O death, that separates those who were
joined, cruel and harsh in forcing apart those who were tied
by friendship! Now, now is your strength destroyed. Now is
that wicked yoke of yours broken by Him who sternly threatened you in the words of Osee: "O death, I will be thy bite!"[9]
So let us with the apostle voice our taunt: "O death, where is
thy victory? O death, where is thy sting?"[10] He who conquered
you has redeemed us—He who betrayed His beloved soul
into the hands of the wicked, that those once wicked He
might make His beloved.[11]

There is much that should be unfolded from Divine Scripture for our common consolation, but we should be satisfied
with the hope of resurrection and by turning our eyes to the
glory of our Redeemer, in whom we believe through faith that
we have already arisen, in the words of the apostle: "Now if
we have died with Christ, we believe that we shall also live
together with him."[12] Wherefore I beseech you, as Christians,
as women of wisdom, to be consoled yourselves, and not to
allow your orphaned daughters to perish with lamenting. For
the wise man seven days of mourning is sufficient,[13] after the
example of the present world, which daily runs in this number.

Therefore, be consoled in the Lord and in the omnipotence
of His power, who "watches over the fatherless and the

---

8 Jerome, *Letter* 75.1 (CSEL 55.30).
9 Cf. Osee 13.14.
10 1 Cor. 15.55.
11 The whole paragraph is based on Jerome, *Letter* 60.2 (CSEL 54.530);
   Letter 60.13 (CSEL 54.563); *Letter* 75.1 (CSEL 55.29-30).
12 Cf. Rom. 6.8.
13 Cf. Ecclus. (Sir.) 22.11.

widow,"[14] who rules all with His grace, who "executes justice for the orphan and the widow,"[15] who "renders justice to the afflicted and the destitute,"[16] lest we seem to have placed our faith in man rather than in God.

I know how you will be tortured by the recollection of the greatness you have lost in him, for one has lost a son, the other has lost a husband; but we too have lost a friend. What can we do, "for all flesh is as grass, and all the glory of the world as the flower of grass"?[17] If this is the will, or rather because this is the will of the Creator (as the apostle said: "The sun rose with a burning heat, and parched the grass, and its flowers fell off"[18]), His will should be dear to us, for it is wrong to refuse it and impious not to follow it. Doubtless, His will and not ours shall remain firm and unchanging, for we are not ours, but His who redeemed us; our will should always depend upon His will. This is why we pray: "Thy will be done."[19]

Therefore, at the time of death, we must say with Job: "The Lord gave, and the Lord has taken away; blessed be the name of the Lord."[20] Let us say this with Job now, lest in the present case we shall later be judged different from him.

Now, it is time for me to stop, lest you become tired of reading. In conclusion, I pray Almighty God to heal you with His consolation, to guard your lives, and to show me in your letters the relief of your sorrow. Now, send Hermenfred to me; when he has visited, he may return to you. Explicit.

---

14 Cf. Ps. 145.9.
15 Deut. 10.18.
16 Ps. 81.3.
17 Cf. 1 Peter 1.24.
18 Cf. James 1.11.
19 Matt. 6.10.
20 Job 1.21.

LETTER 20

Braulio to his honored daughters Hojo and Eutrocia.[1]

I hear that you are not consoled after "seven days."[2] You should have laid aside your grief, since "great piety towards one's own is impiety towards God."[3] You act against the will of the Creator if you mourn without limit, for we shall soon hasten to Hugnan, though he will not return to us, and so we must treat him as absent, not give him up as dead, so that we may appear to be waiting for him, not to have lost him.[4] I pray you not to arouse the anger of God against you; lay aside your grief; be consoled, lest you fall into despair. For it is not right to mourn with personal obstinacy for that which is the common lot of all. Overcome with all your power, even with more power than you possess, the softness of your hearts, and check your freely-flowing tears, for no Christian should be pleased with what is not pleasing to Christ. I have already mentioned his name at mass before the altar of God and have commended his soul to the all-powerful Christ. I hear you have done the same. I have commended him to the Creator, Christ the Lord, who created him and who has taken him away. He has done what He wanted with His work. "For who shall say to him: 'What have you done?' or who can oppose His decree?"[5] "Dare the clay say to its modeler, why have you done so?"[6] when He has the power to mold when He wishes and to break when He wishes? God created you with power to reason; recover your reason, for your affliction cannot accomplish anything for him. Watch, lest in acting against God's will you make Him properly angry with you and perhaps even indignant towards Hugnan.

---

1 Written not long after *Letter* 19.
2 Ecclus. (Sir.) 22.11; cf. *Letter* 19 n. 13.
3 Jerome, *Letter* 39.6 (CSEL 54.306).
4 Cf. *Letter* 15, p. 42.
5 Cf. Wisd. 12.12.
6 Cf. Isa. 45.9.

All that remains is that you should be consoled and pray daily before God for his repose, for that is what we are doing also: this is all we may do, we may grieve no more. Therefore, I pray God that He may console you and that you may have more concern for those who are left behind than for him whom you cannot aid. May Almighty God grant you the grace not to offend Him and to lead a quiet life in this world.

LETTER 21

To Pope Honorius, most reverend lord and deserving of the merits of apostolic glory, from all the bishops who have their sees in Spain.[1]

You are performing extremely well and most suitably the duties of your see as it was conferred upon you by God; with holy "care of all the churches,"[2] resplendent in the shining flame and in the mirrors of your doctrine, you are providing a worthy guardianship for the Church of Christ; with the sword of the divine word and the weapon of heavenly zeal, you are confounding those who deride the Lord's tunic; after the fashion of Nehemias,[3] with your energy and your watchfulness, you are cleansing the sacred House of God, our Mother, from wicked transgressors and accursed deserters.

By the inspiration and sacred meditation of the Most High, these facts were already well known to your most glorious

---

1 Written, undoubtedly, by Braulio on behalf of all the bishops assembled at the Sixth Council of Toledo, which convened Jan. 9, 638. It is a reply to a letter now lost from Pope Honorius I, urging the bishops to be more robust for the faith and to be more eager in destroying infidels. There is reference to converted Jews who had been allowed to return to their original faith. The Fourth Council of Toledo (633) in its 57th canon expressed great concern that the Holy See had been reported indulgent toward such relapses. Most Visigothic kings and church officials had been strongly anti-Jewish for more than fifty years.

2 2 Cor. 11.28

3 Cf. 2 Esd. 3.

son, our prince, King Chintila.[4] By the grace of God, your encouragement was brought to him, while he was attending to the performance of his vows, for we, the bishops of all of Spain and of Gallia Narbonensis, had come together in one assembly, when, with Turninus serving as messenger, there was brought to us your decree, in which we were urged to be more robust on behalf of the faith and more eager in wiping out the pernicious heresies of the unfaithful.

O most noble prince and most blessed lord, we confess that herein is at work no human counsel or plan of men, but the ever-foreseeing and nowhere-nodding plan of the almighty Creator. Over so many intervening lands and so many underlying seas,[5] with one manner and with one thought, the quickener of all and the guide of souls has inspired equally the heart of our prince and your own thoughts conformably on behalf of the faith. What else, then, can we understand than that He whose care is over all has with His divine will breathed into both of you what He in the wisdom of His eternity and universality foresees is to the advantage of the Catholic Church?

Therefore, with inexpressible emotion, we render thanks to the Lord, the King of heaven, and we extol His blessed name beyond all the glories of praise. What is greater or more suitable to human nature than to obey the divine precepts, with watchful zeal to restore to the way of salvation the souls of those who have lost hope, by setting up a separate science as rival to their own? We trust that you will not fail to bear the rewards of your crown as you try to make those who are eager even more awake for the faith and to fire with the warmth of the Holy Spirit those who are less fervent.

On our part, we are not wrapped up in such a degree of sloth as to forget our duty or not to be moved by the prospect of the inspiration of heavenly Grace, but, according to the

---

4 Reigned 636-640.
5 Cf. *Letter* 5 n. 14.

demands of the times, we have had a planned distribution of speakers; we would have your blessedness know that the fact that the matter has not been completely settled by now is due to indulgent, rather than negligent or timid action, following the advice of the apostle, who says: "With modesty admonishing those that follow a different wisdom: in case God should give them repentance to know the truth, and they recover themselves from the snares of the devil."[6] Therefore, we desired to act with calculated restraint to influence with Christian blandishments those who could with difficulty be overcome by rigid discipline, and to temper our genuine severity with the continuous and lengthy treatment of preaching.[7]

We do not believe that any harm is done when victory comes from the delay, for nothing is late when the matter is weighed with greater discretion. The unjust arguments used by your holiness to criticize us have absolutely nothing to do with this case, if I may say so; especially that quotation from Isaia (and not from Ezekiel as you stated; although all the prophets prophesy with one spirit), "Dumb dogs, they cannot bark,"[8] does not pertain to us at all, as I have just said, if your blessedness will but consider, for we keep constant watch over the flocks of the Lord[9] at His inspiration; we frighten wolves with our biting and thieves with our barking, for He "who guards Israel neither slumbers nor sleeps"[10] within us. "For his workmanship we are, created in good works, which God has made ready that we may walk in them."[11] In fact, when it was opportune, we did censure transgressors and we did not keep silent when it was our duty to preach. Lest your apostolic highness think we are producing this to excuse our-

---

6 2 Tim. 2.25, 26.
7 Canon 17 of IV Toledo stated that Jews who are converted of their own free will are apt to prove better Christians than those who are forced to accept baptism.
8 Isa. 56.10.
9 Cf. Luke 2.8.
10 Cf. Ps. 120.4.
11 Cf. Eph. 2.10.

selves and not for the sake of the truth, we have deemed it
necessary to send to you the previous decrees[12] along with the
present canons.[13]

Accordingly, most blessed lord and honorable Pope, in that
love which is our special gift from God, with the veneration
which we owe to the Apostolic See and to the honor of your
holiness, we confidently declare with "a good conscience and
faith unfeigned"[14] what are our opinions in this case. We
think that speakers of falsehood considered that your clemency
was open to hear a wrong opinion, for false words are frequently accustomed to spread anonymously and penetrate
unstable minds with their insubstantial nature, so that lies
and stories that have no connection with the truth are fostered
in the heart. Then, because there is no truth to support them,
they must be protected by iniquity in false colors. But since
God destroys "the mouth of those who speak falsely,"[15] we
do not believe that the serpent's deceit has left its impression
on the rock of Peter, which we know was firmly founded by
our Lord Jesus Christ. Although you, most holy one, mindful
of your office, urge us with most sacred exhortation to be
zealous for the propagation of the faith, we do not believe
that the poison of this dreadful lie has found open room
in the kindness of your heart, for we know that it is a mark
of a fine mind to believe lies only with great difficulty. The
story has even been brought to us (it is incredible to us and
cannot possibly be believed) that, by the oracles of the venerable Prince of Rome, baptized Jews have been allowed to
return to the superstition of their own religion. How false
this is, your sanctity best knows. When that clever and insidi-
ous enemy of the human race realizes that all the effort of his
labor is accomplishing nothing, he tries to console the hearts
of the damned with lying rumors, but you, most reverend of

---

12 IV Toledo.
13 V Toledo.
14 1 Tim. 1.5.
15 Cf. Ps. 62.12.

men and most holy of fathers, must carry on with that virtue which makes you strong in the Lord, with the preaching in which you excel, with all your fervent zeal to bring into the lap of the Mother Church, as rapidly as possible and in any way possible, the "enemies of the cross of Christ"[16] and the worshipers of the demons of Antichrist. Both the Orient and the Occident must be instructed by your voice and must realize that they possess the divine support in your aid and must be eager to destroy the perfidy of the wicked. Whereas you call for a second Elias as you punish the unlucky prophets of Baal,[17] and complain that you are the only one to remain tormented by the demands of a greater zeal, you should, instead, listen to the words from above, that there are many left "who have not bowed their knees to Baal."[18] This we mention to your beatitude without being inflated with the spirit of boasting or pride, but as lovers of the truth, that you may know the truth from us with all due humility; we have thought it just to suggest that the truth should stand between us, while vanity deceives the faithless.

Although reason demands that we should reply in detail to each point in your letter, yet, we reply briefly, but, we think, sufficiently, lest your hearing be wearied by too great protraction of our words. A few words are sufficient for a wise man.[19]

More urgently and more insistently, we request your honored holiness that, in addition to mentioning the blessed apostles and all the saints when you offer prayers in the sight of the Lord for the preservation of the whole Church, you see fit to bestow your kindly piety more abundantly on behalf of our own humble unworthiness, that by the smoke of your offering "of aromatical spices, of myrrh, and frankincense"[20] the dregs

---

16 Phil. 3.18.
17 Cf. 3 Kings 18.40.
18 Rom. 11.4.
19 Isidore, *Letter* 8.3 to Eugenius; ultimately from Plautus, *Persa* 729.
20 Cf. Cant. 3.6.

and impurities of our sins may be washed away, lest we receive
"what our deeds deserved"[21] in the present or in future ages,
for we know that no mortal crosses this vast sea without
danger.

Therefore, most excellent and outstanding of bishops, for
the serenity of your son, our prince, and for us and for
the peoples committed to our care, offer before God the aid
of your intercession, which will redound to your sanctity's
eternal glory. In this we, too, offer our assistance, asking the
Almighty Lord to make the present course of His Church
tranquil and quiet in the dignity of a most religious conduct, that the ship of faith, which is constantly threatened
by the rocks of temptations and the Charybdis of pleasures
and the waves of persecutions and the barking of Scylla and
the madness of the Gentiles, may, by His guidance and gov-
ernance, be brought most quietly to a safe harbor, so that
when the sea and the winds have been rebuked,[22] all things
may turn out prosperously for it in response to its prayer
for felicity.

At the end of this letter, we have thought to add something
special of our own to the head of our ministry, namely, that
your apostolic highness should reflect most seriously on the
question whether those who are involved in any crime whatsoever ought to be punished so severely as your beatitude has
decreed those should be condemned who are stained with the
fault of prevarication. We have never seen this done anywhere
by the decrees of our forefathers, nor is it to be found in the
divine words in the pages of the New Testament.

---

21 Luke 23.41.
22 Cf. Luke 8.24.

LETTER 22

Braulio to my lord, Bishop Eutropius.[1]

To the anxious concern of your beatitude, in which you deign to ask a question whose answer, you say, you do not deserve, I cannot render proper thanks; how much less can I reply? But He who alone made Himself a debtor for the poor, and whose concern it is to make answer even to the impossible, will give you answer in my stead, my lord, and will Himself favor you with the same kindness which you show towards me.

Concerning the feast of Easter, as you have questioned my unworthy self, your sanctity should know that this is the truth: Easter this year falls on April 8, the twenty-first day of the moon. That is how our elders of old prescribed, namely, Theophilus to the Emperor Theodosius;[2] likewise, his successor, Cyril;[3] likewise, Dionysius;[4] likewise, Proterius to Pope Leo;[5] and also Paschasinus;[6] and the rest whom it would take too long to mention, though I must add the outstanding man

---

1 Written late in 640. Eutropius has asked Braulio when the next Easter will be celebrated. The date of April 8, as given, and the twenty-first day of the moon coincide only for the year 641. Eutropius would have needed to know the date far enough in advance to be able to inform the priests in his diocese when Lent would begin. The see of Eutropius is unknown, but it must have been near Saragossa. He appears again in *Letter* 37.

2 Prefatory letter of Theophilus, Bishop of Alexandria, to Emperor Theodosius I, written in 338 to accompany a set of paschal tables, printed in B. Krusch, *Studien zur christlichmittelalterlichen Chronologie* (Leipzig 1880) 220-26.

3 St. Cyril of Alexandria, prefatory letter to Theodosius II, accompanying a set of paschal tables for the years 403-512; Krusch, *op. cit.* 88.

4 Probably Dionysius Exiguus, who wrote several works on the paschal cycle. His *Liber de Paschate* quotes from the letter of Proterius mentioned below.

5 Letter of Proterius of Alexandria to Pope Leo the Great; Krusch, *op. cit.* 267-69.

6 Paschasinus, Bishop of Lilybaeum, to Leo the Great on determining the date of Easter in 444; Krusch, *op. cit.* 245-50.

of our day, Isidore of Seville.[7] I think that, in such a large
and important subject, they would not have failed to employ
their customary carefulness and labor.

Now in the table which you, my lord, inspected, as your
sanctity writes, there was probably an error on the part of
the manuscript or of the scribe, and that is why it happens
to be written that way and not as it should be.[8] This year,
the Pasch of the Jews falls on April 1, not that of the Christians, in accordance with the Old rather than the New Testament. Now, theirs must precede and ours must follow, because
the Old Testament comes first and then the New; in accordance with this, our Lord ate the old Passover with his disciples
on the fifth day of the week, and later, by His Passion and Res-
surrection, consecrated for us the Sabbath, which dawns on
Sunday.[9] Therefore, we cannot celebrate with them, for it is
prohibited by the Council of Nicaea, as found in Book Seven
of the *Ecclesiastical History*.[10] Therefore, we must celebrate
Easter on the following Sunday, which, as I have already said,
will be April 8, the twenty-first day of the moon, since the
fourteenth day of the moon is celebrated on their April 1,
the preceding Sunday. Further, the half (fourteenth day)
runs out before the third quarter by our custom, but with

---

7 Isidore, *Etymologies* 6.17.5-9, with paschal cycle for the years 627-721.
   The main reason for quoting these sources, which Braulio may have
   possessed in a single collection of *computus*, was to cite Alexandrian
   authority, to which the Roman Church had once violently objected,
   that if the fourteenth day of the moon fell on Sunday, then Easter
   must be celebrated on the following Sunday, even though it might
   come after April 21. Other sources enforce the requirement there
   stated that the Christian Easter may not be observed at the same time
   as the Jewish Passover. For a full discussion, see C. W. Jones,
   Bedae Opera de Temporibus (Cambridge, Mass. 1943) 18-22.
8 Most of the two preceding sentences was taken directly from the
   letter of Proterius just mentioned.
9 "Quod in dominica lucescit" is a difficult phrase.
10 Braulio must have had the Latin translation by Rufinus of the
   History of Eusebius. The paschal canons which it contains in 7.32 are,
   however, said to be those of Anatolius of Laodicea, rather than the
   Acts of Nicaea.

them the half is left vacant, because they do not celebrate the Passover until the fourteenth day of the moon is complete.[11]

To satisfy you briefly, our Lord Jesus Christ, who came "not to destroy the law, but to fulfill,"[12] "for the consummation of the law is Christ,"[13] first determined Easter by law and consummated it with these words: "I will not drink from henceforth of this fruit of the vine."[14] Afterwards, to start the new and separate it from the old, that the old and the new might not be confused in one, He began thus: "This cup is the new covenant in my blood";[15] and that the distinction might also be observed by us, He pointed to the difference, saying: "Do this in remembrance of me."[16]

Lo, I have sent you, my lord, a few brief thoughts as they occurred to me, but I would not be reputed verbose nor overabundant; for what I said is not mine alone, since truth is common to all. Therefore, if I have said anything worthy, let it be considered a gift of God, concerning which you rightly presume more of what we all share in common. If the truth speaks anything through me, then, it is yours rather than mine, for you love truth more than I; and since "every good gift is from above,"[17] it is, accordingly, more yours, because you are His who is above. If, on the other hand, there is anything in these words which is displeasing to reason, it is mine and not God's; in the same way, when we speak truths, they are God's not ours. Therefore, they belong more to him who is His rather than his own; and when you find in me what is His, you find your own, and in me you possess the things of Him to whom belong the things which you possess.

---

11 I.e., the Jews actually commence Passover at sunset and use the fifteenth day of the moon.
12 Matt. 5.17.
13 Rom. 10.4.
14 Matt. 26.29.
15 Luke 22.20.
16 Luke 22.19.
17 James 1.17.

Finally, I add a reverent and loving greeting, and entrust my salvation to your prayers.

LETTER 23

Braulio, humble servant of the saints of God, to my lord and bishop Valentinus, one with me in spirit.[1]

We were pleased and delighted to receive the letter from your holiness, especially since it is a pledge of your affection and a proof of your good health, so that there is opportunity, which, I confess to you, is pleasant for me, of returning this mutual pledge of love. Since we believe that nothing happens in the ordered course of events without our Creator, we, in our turn, offer thanks as great as our heart can feel, greater than our tongue can express. I think nothing worthier can be said, nothing shorter heard, nothing happier thought, nothing more profitable understood or done, of all the things that we bear in our hearts and speak with our mouths and write with our pens, than "Thanks to God."

I have read your letter and am so overcome by your blandishments that I feel myself oppressed rather than uplifted[2] by the tally of all the services which you consider I have performed for you, for we think that we possess little or nothing of what your benevolence ascribes to us. Even if there is any truth in what has been said on my behalf, it must be referred to Him "from whom is every best gift,"[3] from whom also comes

---

1 Written between 641 and 646. The recipient may be the same as Anianus, Bishop of Valencia in 646, but I am inclined to believe with Risco that *unianimus* is not a proper name, but an adjective referring to their common friendship, used here but not in the address to *Letter* 24, especially as Lynch (p. 69) has called attention to the use of "una anima tua et mea" near the end of the letter. Even so, the latter could be Braulio's natural word play on a proper name Unianimus.
2 Jerome, *Letter* 47.1 (CSEL 54.345).
3 Cf. James 1.17.

the gift that you never receive anything but kind answers from anyone. You, my lord, both display and describe your love towards us, but I beg you not to be deceived by love, although you seem to place that love, not only in what you write, but also in your heart. Accordingly, although I am not unaware that I am your debtor, if I return your praises, I shall not be lying, but I fear to speak quite superfluously, when I mention those truths about you of which no one is unaware. I have spared your sense of shame, lest I show that I was ashamed when you praised me, so that your own extreme modesty might overcome its conscience.

But what shall I do? It is written: "Pay your debts"[4] and "owe no man anything,"[5] but in this I prefer to be a debtor rather than one who repays, lest you think that I want to hear the same about myself and hasten once again to repay your debt to me. Wherefore I request that when I enjoy your praises, I may be allowed to feel the rewards of your prayers rather than to hear my own kindnesses undeservingly enumerated.

Lo, I have answered you on the spur of the moment, inflamed with the love of charity, so that the very prolixity of my tardy reply satisfies my longing for you, when I answer much of little consequence to your few but important words, for whatever I pour out in writing rather than speak is done as though I were talking with you face to face.

Since you are my other soul, or rather your soul and mine are one in Christ, I pray and beseech that your prayers to God for me be incessant and that you not think that I have any merit, lest you shame yourself by your intervention for me, thinking that I have what I do not have, instead of praying that I should be what you perhaps think I am; for if you examine the secrets of my actions, you will find more in me

---

4 Cf. Rom. 13.7.
5 Rom. 13.8.

that you would wish to suppress, than what would cause you to rejoice when you have finished your prayer.

All pretext aside, I pray I may deserve to be inspired by a letter from you, I pray earnestly on your behalf, and I append a wish for your most ample health, as though I were in your presence.

LETTER 24

Braulio, unworthy servant of the saints of God, to my lord, Bishop Valentinus.[1]

You may be sure that I labor with extreme vexation under the same storms and tempests that you complain of as disturbing your repose. What can be safe for those for whom the end of the world has come, when in what I may call the trembling old age of this earth, when it has been struck by the most violent maladies, we find that we are more afflicted by its ills and falls than refreshed by the repose of its maturity and nobility? We must take refuge in Him in whom is all power and control of the universe, that He may not give us what we really deserve, but may with His customary mercy lighten our burdens and our tribulations. From His clemency we may presume that, while we are still in this body, He will give us the opportunity of seeing you and of receiving you and enjoying your blessing, that what we greatly desire, we may one day receive with our eyes. For although the absence of the body does not separate those whom an equal oneness in the Lord joins, since wherever we are we are one in Him who is everywhere, for we love Him only and, in Him, our neighbor; still, since we consist of body and soul, it is a far greater benefit in this swiftly passing life to see one whom you long for than to long for one whom you see. Inspired by this

---

1 Written between 641 and 646. Although the opening pessimism is full of commonplaces, it may refer to political difficulties in the first years of Chindaswinth, 642 and later.

kind of love, we mutually long for one another and mutually greet one another.

I constantly express my gratitude to your worthiness, whose love is so strong that it sends for news; I ask pardon for my negligence which does not send for news as it should, since the men of this territory are frightened to go there on account of robbers. I humbly pray that you do not repay me in kind, but whenever you find an opening, send me an advice of your safety.

LETTER 25

Braulio, unworthy servant of the saints of God, to my lord Emilian, priest and abbot.[1]

Although we are assailed on all sides by the continuous seething resulting from the revolving of the earth, you are placed by divine favor in an order of events to the plentiful profit of souls; therefore, I have noted that the anchor of your mind is founded upon such a solid heavenly rock that, no matter in what ways the world may rage and the sea swell and these mighty swirling waters lift their heads, your mind cannot be completely destroyed nor swallowed by Charybdis nor devoured by Scylla's barking dogs[2] nor softened by the song of the Sirens. Therefore, rightly has Verity spoken of such a wise man: "Because you have built your house upon a rock, the rain fell, the floods came, the winds blew, and beat against that house, but it did not fall, because it was founded on rock."[3]

Why all this? Because I have been thinking about the efforts of your dedicated labor and the toil of your calm mind

---

1 Written between 642 and 646 to Emilian, not to be confused with the saint whose life Braulio composed. This Emilian appears to have been, for a short while, a counselor of King Chindaswinth in Toledo.
2 Cf. *Letter* 21, p.
3 Cf. Matt. 7.24, 25.

on behalf of all, and the fact that you are situated on a
double road, so to speak, tolerating the vexations of the present
world in proportion to the multiplicity of good deeds, and
procuring the rewards of holy zeal by holy conduct. Now,
I do not bring this up in the manner of flattery nor with deceptive blandishments, for one who flatters may be pleasant,
but still is to be considered an enemy;[4] rather, I have made
this beginning in order to strengthen your mind to be consoled for temptations and to withstand the storms without
which one cannot live, that adversity may be bravely endured and prosperity avoided, and that we may so carefully
walk a middle course that the labors of this present life may
be practice, not destruction for us. Since you have been so
kind as to become my supporter and I do not doubt that you
are a part of my soul, likewise, my concern for you is as great
as if it were for myself, the Lord knows. Hence, I commend
this your humble servant to your kindness that he may be
presented through you to our glorious lord [the king] and
may by your care be instructed how he should proceed.

I have been looking for and cannot find the book of
Apringius, Bishop of Beja, which is a *Commentary on the
Apocalypse.*[5] I am asking you to get the text and send it to
me to be copied, for it will be easy for you on account of
your widespread power and the large size of your city, even
if you do not have it, to find out from whom it may be obtained so that you can send it to us. I know that, at one time,
it did exist in the library of Count Laurentius. You, my lord,
must find it wherever it is and fulfill my petition, for it will
be copied and returned immediately.

Finally, I add with full devotion the obsequies of your
servant as an offering to you, and I am anxiously desirous of

---

4 Jerome, *Letter* 22.2 (CSEL 54.146).
5 Written about a century before Braulio's time and known to Isidore.
From a copy written in Barcelona in the eleventh or twelfth century,
two large fragments have survived at Copenhagen; first edited in 1900:
no. 1093 in Dekkers, *Clavis patrum latinorum.* Obviously, the commentary was never widely dispersed.

being constantly favored with the words from your most learned pen.

LETTER 26

The sinner Emilian to my lord, Bishop Braulio.[1]

Since I am unable to express in words the dutiful feelings of my heart in thanking you, my lord, for the favor of your kindness and grace, when you deigned to admonish freely and to instruct with salutary advice my unworthy self, I use all my prayers and supplications to ask God to return the favor to you. I would ask your influence, my lord, that, by your merits and prayers before God, you deign to have accomplished in me the special praises and advice which you have offered, that I may deserve to obtain with your blessing what is pleasing both to our God and to your mind.

As for the book which you bade me search for and send to your beatitude, God is my witness that I did my very best to find it, and when I could not find it anywhere else, I mentioned it to your son, our lord [the king], and he had his library searched, but the manuscript was not to be found anywhere. We even made inquiries about the books of Laurentius, but because, as you know, his property had been scattered on that occasion, we could not investigate that source.

I pay you the reverent dues of my servitude and commend myself for protection and encouragement to the sanctuary of your mind, and quite humbly beg that, whenever the occasion arises, I may deserve to be informed of your own prosperity by a letter from you.

---

1 Written between 642 and 646 in reply to *Letter* 25.

LETTER 27

Braulio, humble servant of the saints of God, to my lord Emilian, priest and abbot.[1]

If I could have deserved to be informed of your arrival, if I could have known your route or the time or even a designated place where I might have visited with you, I should not have incurred this fault [of not entertaining you]. Though I was not aware of any of these things, God knows that I desire to be presented in your presence, yet do not know how it can be done. If both of these should become possible, please do not refuse to see my humble self, for whose redemption the Redeemer of the human race made Himself visible, "taking our infirmities."[2] If it be not possible, I ask you to pray for miserable me and not to think differently of me than if I had been allowed to receive you most courteously, for, both in body and soul, I am your client and your slave and I might have been your servant anywhere; I say this without reservation before God. But ecstasy "is spiritual and I am carnal,"[3] sold under the reproach of infirmity; for this, my desire is spiritual, but, on the other hand, the support of my ecstasy is corruptible. Therefore, discord is concord, and concord discord, and we are so borne down by miseries that "what we wish, we do not; and what we do not wish, that we do."[4] But it is sufficient, when the listener is wise, to announce the result and take note of the impossibility.

Finally, I commend myself and all things delegated to me and request that you be propitious to us and deign to guard us, not only by your prayers, but also by your exalted protection.

---

1 Written between 642 and 646, probably some time later than *Letters* 25 and 26. Emilian has made a visit to Saragossa that Braulio was not informed of.
2 Cf. Matt. 8.17.
3 Cf. Rom. 7.14.
4 Cf. Rom. 7.19.

LETTER 28

Braulio, unworthy servant of the saints of God, to my lord Ataulfus.[1]

I have heard that your mother-in-law, the lady Mello, has departed from this life. I think you must be in mourning, as you have a Christian soul, but you must display your grief in such a way as to console your wife and her brother. A prudent man displays fortitude in bearing present ills and concealing adversity. It is proper for you, dearest lord, to use that courage in which you excel to offer such consolation to your family that you will not show how crushed with pain you yourself are; not that you should not grieve at all, for even the apostle rejoiced at the bringing back to life of Epaphras and would have been grieved at the death of him whose resurrection brought him joy.[2] Although one who is overcome by his own sobbing is not the best person to offer consolation,[3] still, you must guide the ship of your soul on this doubtful journey in such a way as to offer solace to the sorrowing without providing your enemies an opportunity to boast.

In conclusion, I salute you with all humility and reverence, and pray that the divine piety may deign to save you in all His grace.

---

1 Written between 642 and 646; two of the Visigothic counts at the Eighth Council of Toledo in 653 had the name Ataulfus.
2 Cf. Phil. 2.25-28; *Letter* 15 n. 4.
3 Cf. *Letters* 15 n. 8, and 19 n. 2.

LETTER 29

Braulio, unworthy servant of the saints of God, to his illustrious lords and beloved children in Christ, Gundeswinda and Givarius.[1]

He more rightly bewails the miseries of human life who expects that he will die each day;[2] hence, it is not so much having departed from the world as having lived with the world that is full of sadness. Moreover, living so as to serve Christ is to have conquered the world and not to have lived with the world, which we believe your mother of sacred memory has done, and for this she is to be congratulated that she is without temptations, even if she has left us in various misfortunes. For the passing of Christians, no doubt, is joy, of which the apostle says: "Do not grieve, even as others who have no hope";[3] and again: "For to me to live is Christ and to die is gain."[4] But if our hope is our Redeemer, in whom we are given victory over death and the glory of resurrection, there is no reason why we should deplore the fate of those whom we know to have died well. Therefore, be consoled in the Lord and in the omnipotence of His virtue, who can be our refuge and a resting-place for travelers. Do not mourn for what you have lost, but rejoice that you have sent your mother ahead to eternal life.[5] For there, those who precede us await our arrival. With the favor of God, may that arrival be such as to gladden, not only them, but even the angels of peace.

Why do I protract this? The river of mortality cannot

---

1 Written between 642 and 646 to console this noble couple, probably a sister and brother, on the death of their mother. The second name was printed as Agivarius by Risco. Since Madoz does not mention a variant, one must suppose that the manuscript has Givarius.

2 Cf. Jerome, *Letter* 53.11 (CSEL 54.465); *Letter* 54.18 (*ibid*. 485).

3 1 Thess. 4.13.

4 Phil. 1.21.

5 Cf. Jerome, *Letter* 123.10 (CSEL 56.84); the word play on *amitto* and *praemitto* is a commonplace found in several Christian writings.

stand still; it runs and carries us along with it, and so we must bear all that our situation brings us, exposed as we are to sin. Even the Savior came subject to death; although He referred to Lazarus as sleeping,[6] and likewise the girl,[7] still He said as He drank the troubled bitterness of this torrent: "My soul is sad, even unto death."[8] This He said for us, not for Himself.

Since there is nothing that can ward off the inevitable torture of this evil, it is necessary to tolerate patiently what no man can escape. It is not the first time nor the last that this has happened to us; if it were the first, we should say that it should have begun with another; if it were the last, we should complain that it ought to have ceased with another so that somehow it could have kept away from us. But since, as I have already said, no one's foot is free from the seduction of this snare, let us do what we should as Christians: let us bear the evil and hope for the good; let us be refreshed by love; let us "take pride in the Lord";[9] let us be consoled in Christ, and let us follow His teaching, as He would have us do. He is able to give her rest and us aid, her the kingdom and us the government.

LETTER 30

Braulio, unworthy servant of the saints of God, to my lord Wistremir.[1]

Although one who is ruled by his own sobbing does not offer

---

6 Cf. John 11.11.
7 Cf. Matt. 9.24.
8 Matt. 26.38.
9 1 Cor. 1.31.

---

1 Written between 642 and 646 to console a Gothic noble after the death of his wife. Braulio calls her "sister," but blood relationship is not at all certain.

the best consolation,[2] still, I would have borne all the grief we have in common, if only I might hear that you are consoled. The dreadful news had already penetrated me, and was but renewed and again brought to life by your letter.

Alas, O bitter terms of death; without Christ is all our life vain.[3] The tears escape, the very life is oppressed with heaviness, my dictation quavers, and for grief the words do not come in correct order. She has gone, she has gone whom we loved, in whom you had the ties of love and all consolation, while to me she brought distinction and was an example of charity. She was your glory, our praise, your ornament, and our source of exultation. Who would believe that she would depart so early in life, when she appeared to be God's provision for your old age, to refresh you when weary and to comfort you when anxious amid the cares of the world? But what we did not expect has occurred and what we did not even think of has come. Alas for mortal life, daily becoming empty for the living!

What can we do, since such is the condition of mortals? Let us be consoled in the Lord, in whom is the consolation of a far better life and, as true faith holds, let us not cease to hope that she has been carried to a better place and released from the misery of this life. I doubt if one could find a single person who enjoys living in the face of all the evils that constantly arise; if one could, he would prove to be either foolish or stupid. Therefore, since our Creator and Redeemer, who both sees the future and holds the present, has seen what was best for her soul, I think she was carried away because He loved her, and "lest wickedness of the world should pervert her mind";[4] "sufficient for the day is its own trouble."[5] Therefore, let us rejoice, rather than mourn; not because we

---

2 Cf. *Letters*, 15 n. 9, 19 n. 2, 28 n. 3, 34 n. 9.
3 Jerome, *Letter* 60.13 (CSEL 54.564).
4 Cf. Wisd. 4.11.
5 Cf. Matt. 6.34.

have lost, but because we have had such a one,[6] you a wife and I a sister.

Because it is a part of your wisdom to live in such a way that you will not incur reproof from your enemies, be consoled and magnanimously avoid grief; to express it very briefly, you should hold within yourself both love for her who is gone and a reasonable consolation. I think that will become easier as time passes, but you must begin now, for everything that is thought over and meditated frequently becomes easier, no matter how dreadful it may seem. Therefore, most illustrious of men, use all your efforts to console yourself and your family; at her death, you must not forget those whom you and she both loved, lest you seem to have lost the affection you had through her when she was alive.

May Almighty God fill your heart with His Grace and take away your sorrow and allow you, after a long time, to share immortal life with her.

LETTER 31

A petition

Braulio, humble servant of the saints of God and your servant, to our glorious King Chindaswinth.[1]

Almighty God, in whose likeness reign the good powers of

---

6 Cf. Braulio, *Letter* 29; also Jerome, *Letter* 108.1 (CSEL 55.306).

---

1 Four of the letters from Braulio to the king and Eugene's letter to Braulio are preceded by the word *suggerendum* to indicate a petition. This one may be dated in 646, because Bishop Eugene I of Toledo died in that year and the king used the lay sanction, then customary in Spain, to appoint as his successor Eugene II, long a faithful deacon and archdeacon of Braulio in Saragossa. Braulio's strong objections here confirm the statement of Ildefonse that the appointment was somewhat "violent." The closeness of Eugene's relationship to Braulio is shown by several epitaphs which he composed for members of Braulio's family and other poems honoring familiar scenes in Saragossa.

this world, is persuaded by the prayers of suppliants, is moved to pity by the sight of misfortunes, restores to consolation those afflicted with desolation. He had mercy on the people of Ninive,[2] He had respect for the misfortunes of Sedecia,[3] He was propitiated and spared the afflictions of Achab,[4] though he was wicked. Therefore, most holy prince, I request that you, at long last, have pity on me, afflicted, wretched, asking a remedy, denuded of my solace, deprived of my counsel, oppressed by weakness and infirmity, whose life being set in bitterness would rather enter the state of death than breathe the breath of this present life.

I had at least one comfort of my life, though I was in the midst of many adversities, the sight of your servant, Eugene, my archdeacon. Although the numerous vicissitudes of the church in which we had been so unworthily chosen embittered my heart, still, we would have refuge in the words of God that "not by bread alone does man live,"[5] which is not undeservingly understood as an aid to this life, and we would be refreshed in every word of God, for it is written: "A brother that helps a brother shall be exalted";[6] and: "Iron sharpens iron, so man sharpens the countenance of his friend."[7]

But now, by the command of your majesty, a part of my life is being taken away from me and I do not know what I shall do in this life. I am being blinded by the loss of the light of my body, my courage wavers, I am destitute of sense; hence, I direct my prayers that you do not separate him from me, that so you may not be separated from the kingdom of heaven and your seed may possess your kingdom. Now, truly, as I faithfully beseech, I do not see how he can accomplish anything great there, but his absence in this city of yours may

2 Cf. Jona 3.10.
3 Cf. Jer. 32.4, 5.
4 Cf. 3 Kings 21.29.
5 Matt. 4.4.
6 Cf. Prov. 18.19.
7 Cf. Prov. 27.17.

cause much harm, for, as I have mentioned, my health is poor; he had been trained for everything, to make announcements from the pulpit, to carry out your orders, and to help on any occasion in many ways.

To you, most pious prince, we confess all. May He who sees our secret and hidden thoughts, who is concerned for our troubles, so inspire your heart that you may arrange the affairs of one church without making another destitute.

LETTER 32

His excellency to the holy and venerable father, Bishop Braulio.[1]

We have received your eloquent petition, adorned with most flowery words and equipped with all verbal euphonies, which your holiness has had sent to our clemency. In it, we have studied your carefully expressed thoughts and are given to know in compressed, but easily understood language, in few words, but not without wisdom, that you wish the arch-deacon Eugene to be retained with you.

You ask our majesty with effusive prayers and firm intent that he may be released to you, but your holiness could hardly have supposed that that could happen, when the mind of our serene lord is most ardently anxious to promote him to this honor, for Almighty God, whose commandment every creature obeys,[2] "blows where he will"[3] until He fulfills His good pleasure, that he may come to offer sacrifice to please his Creator. The preeminent piety of the Lord has already foreknown whom He desires to be predestined for the better.[4] Therefore,

---

1 A reply to *Letter* 31, containing a polite and formal negative answer. Lynch plausibly suggests that it was composed by the Emilian of *Letters* 25-27.
2 Cf. Wisd. 19.6.
3 John 3.8.
4 Cf. Rom. 8.29.

if those things persist in the will of God, as we trust, we cannot do other than what He wills, nor is our justice to be pretermitted at your petition, since he is a native of this place in which we now desire to create him bishop.

Therefore since justice lies on our side, no doubt, the things that are promised to our devotion, that are to be pleasing to Christ, shall not be suppressed. Your beatitude must not take this unkindly, for from this experience the greatest reward can be won before the Lord, provided you offer him to be sacrificed to God as a bishop. Praise of you will become even higher in the divine presence, if the Holy Catholic Church shall have been lighted from your teachings.

Therefore, most blessed man, since you do not believe that I can do other than what is pleasing to God, it is necessary that you accede to our exhortation and surrender this Archdeacon Eugene to be bishop of our church.

LETTER 33

A petition

Braulio, unworthy servant of the saints of God and your servant, to our most glorious lord, King Chindaswinth.[1]

Although the chain of the ties by which I was joined in the Lord with your servant, the Archdeacon Eugene, has been temporarily separated rather than broken, still I have sent him to your presence, as commanded by your excellency, not without the hope of that piety with which you have been wont to regard the miserable and succor the afflicted; namely, that you may restore him to your patron, Saint Vincent,[2] in that office which he held until now. If, however, the providence of the divine disposition turns the heart of your

1 Written in 646 as a reply to *Letter* 32.
2 Eugene had apparently been assigned to the Basilica of St. Vincent in Saragossa.

clemency from our prayer, then I must give him up as mortal will determines. Until the ordination given by your excellency is accomplished, I commend with all my powers of prayer his lamentable transfer.

LETTER 34

Braulio, unworthy servant of the saints of God, to my lord and special son in Christ, Nebridius.[1]

This fugitive life, vain as smoke, promising and deceptive, deceiving before it has fulfilled what it promised, is nothing at all, as we learn from wise and prudent men of whom you are one, and as can daily be seen with eyes that fail as the times themselves do.

It has come to me that my daughter, your wife—most dear to both of us, alas!—has departed from this life. I bewail the lot of human life in ourselves more than in her as I wonder and sigh at what may happen to us. Meanwhile, our consolation is in the Lord, our Redeemer, since by His death He conquered death that He, in whose power lay our life and death, may Himself be our defense against the power of a second death, He who alone was able to penetrate hell and conquer the pains of death and, after the third day, to return to the upper world. Hoping in this, we do not weaken in faith, because His "kindness shall encompass them who trust in the Lord."[2]

You also know that your wife held this faith and we are certainly well aware of it because she was and we are Christians. In the anchor of this stability, we are advised by the apostle to be consoled, when he says: "I would not have you ignorant concerning those that are asleep, lest you should

---

1 Written in 646 or 647 to Nebridius, otherwise unknown, on the occasion of his wife's death.
2 Cf. Ps. 31.10.

grieve, even as others who have no hope."[3] Life is not taken away from Christians, but is changed for the better. That is why the dead are called "sleeping," according to what the Lord said in the Gospel concerning Lazarus: "Lazarus, our friend, sleeps."[4] At the resurrection of the faithful, this sleep will be the fulfillment of life; so, since we are Christians, we should be consoled, not in ourselves, but in Him "who raises the dead and gives them life."[5]

I believe that this regeneration is already your consolation, but present desolation affects the heart amid the precepts of virtue and the hope of resurrection.[6] If we had been the first to experience this or were thought to be the last, we would say: "Why has this not happened before us, or why will it not happen after us?" Let our consolation, then, be that we are neither the first nor the last to experience death.[7] Since all the world is the same and we must daily fear the same fate ourselves: "Let us win our souls by our patience,"[8] and let us have the endurance which should be in the Christian soul; let grief cease where there is no remedy and let us pour out our souls in the sight of Him who is rest for the deceased and the mercy of revelation for the living.

But why should I speak to you at length, since one whose grief overcomes him in this case can hardly be the proper one to offer consolation.[9] Both you and I should be consoled by patience in the Lord and by the hope that we may hope for better things and that we may endure what overtakes us. I ask Him in whose power is both present and future life to give her repose, and to deign to impart to us salvation in Him.[10]

---

3 Cf. 1 Thess. 4.13.
4 John 11.11.
5 Cf. John 5.21.
6 Jerome, *Letter* 60.2 (CSEL 54.550).
7 Cf. *Letters* 19 and 29.
8 Cf. Luke 21.19.
9 Cf. *Letters* 15 n. 9, 19 n. 2, 28 n. 3, 30 n. 2.
10 The letter in the manuscript ends with a phrase which seems to belong elsewhere: "Many things occurred to me to write to your charity."

LETTER 35

A petition

Eugene, your humble servant, to my lord and truly my master, Bishop Braulio.[1]

Two situations have arisen in my church which have caused my soul exceeding grief and all my knowledge has found no remedy to apply except to ask your advice.

We have learned of a brother who, without receiving the rank of priest, is performing the office of priest. To make you better acquainted with the case, I shall mention all the details. This same brother caused much trouble for my lord Eugene.[2] When Eugene was asked by the king to ordain this brother a priest, he could not disobey the command of the prince, so hit upon the following scheme. He led him to the altar, made no imposition of the hand, and, while the clerics were singing loudly, he pronounced a malediction over him instead of a benediction,[3] as he later confessed to persons worthy of trust and very close to him, conjuring them to silence while he lived. Inform me speedily what your prudence desires to have done in this case, for I do not know if he is considered to be a priest or if they who were baptized and anointed with chrism[4] by him are rightly called Christians. Solve this problem about which I am so much in doubt; may Christ in the same way loose the bond of your sin, if you have any.

Likewise, we have heard that in certain places deacons anoint with chrism, and I do not know what we should do

---

1 Probably written in 647, soon after Eugene became Bishop of Toledo.
2 Eugene I, Bishop of Toledo 636-646. Ildefonse says that he had a deacon named Lucidius who was overfond of worldly things and seized much booty by violence. Risco suggests the identity of Lucidius with the improperly ordained priest.
3 Cf. Gen. 27.12.
4 There is much discussion of whether the chrism is confirmation itself or merely a rite after baptism. Lynch, *op. cit.* 89-94, strongly supports the latter view; this translation is indebted throughout to his detailed study of this letter and the next.

about those who have been anointed with chrism by them.
Should the unction with holy chrism be repeated? Or if it is
not repeated, is it taken for chrism, which may have been
presumptuously done under pressure or perpetrated in ignorance? I request your piety to inform me what I should do
about it.

Now that I have mentioned the two matters, a third occurs
to me. Some priests, against the law and the ancient canons,
presume to anoint the baptized with chrism which they themselves have made, if such is to be called chrism.[5] I confess I do
not know what remedy or correction can be offered those so
anointed.

I ask you to enlighten me about these matters, for you
bask in the brighter light of divine wisdom. You continually
meditate upon the holy law, you zealously pursue, ardently
follow, and cleverly destroy the shady intrigues of wicked
hearts, while I, if I ever did possess a tiny vein of meager
knowledge that I could modestly apply, have been so completely drained of it by pressing ills and innumerable storms
of care that I can produce not so much as a drop. I beseech
you, by Him through whose gift you are blessed and by whose
instruction you have proved yourself learned and skilled, that,
by the sacred commands from your lips, you immediately
instruct me concerning these matters.

LETTER 36

*Braulio, unworthy servant of the saints of God, to Eugene,
in a special way my lord and my primate of bishops.*[1]

If huge numbers of cares did not surround me, if the

---

5 Both the First Council of Toledo in 400 and the Second Council of
   Seville in 619 forbade priests to make chrism, and Braulio also answers
   that it must be blessed by a bishop.

---

1 Written in 647 as an answer to *Letter* 35.

world's wickedness did not involve me in its storms, if the riotousness of the envious barking against me were silent, and if the solitude in which I am deservingly swallowed did not frighten me, I still could not return the easy answer which you want to your questions, which I have never heard nor experienced before, for it is an unknown matter that disturbs the mind and could not have the easy answer afforded to matter previously foreseen or long meditated. I realize, however, that your wise foresight desires to try out in me something which cannot trouble me and may show that I have a wisdom lacking in others. I sense your good intentions, but I am not aware of my abilities. What can we possess, however small, that you extol with the praise of a learned voice to such an extent that you compel a lazy, forgetful old man to reach for the heights, that you involve a veteran, and, unfortunately, an ancient one, in these questions in which ignorance is dangerous and knowledge is presumptuous? Since, however, the one Master and heavenly Teacher, who teaches men knowledge, says: "Without me you can do nothing, but with me you will be able to do everything";[2] and again, the prophet: "The Lord shall give the word";[3] and again: "Open wide your mouth, and I will fill it";[4] therefore, in accordance with your request, in accordance with my duty to obey, in accordance with the hope of divine promise, in accordance with the fact that nothing is impossible to a believer, I shall try to speak as best I can, and to tell you, if I shall be able to discover anything, just as He commanded me to minister who rules His own Church, and I shall reveal it to you, my lord, in a plausible manner. It will then be your task to use the discretion in which you are strong, the care in which you excel, and the instruction which is your strongest asset to take my remarks and approve what is right, correct what is wrong, cover up what is improper, and publish what is proper.

---

2 Cf. John 15.5.
3 Cf. Ps. 67.12.
4 Ps. 80.11.

Now, then, let us turn to the topics themselves. You
say in your letter that two situations have arisen in your
church which have caused your soul exceeding grief and that
all your knowledge has found no remedy to apply. You write
of a certain brother who, without receiving the rank of priest,
is performing the office of priest, and to explain the whole
case, you relate that he caused much trouble for your predecessor, who was asked by the king to ordain this brother a
priest. Because he could not disobey the command of the
prince, to use your words, he hit upon the following scheme.
He led him to the altar, made no imposition of the hand on
him, and, while the clerics were singing loudly, he pronounced
a malediction instead of a benediction, as this predecessor of
yours later confessed to persons worthy of trust and very
close to him, conjuring them to silence while he lived. Then,
you ask me to consider what should be done in this case,
because you say you do not know whether he should be
considered to be a priest or whether they who were anointed
with chrism by him are rightly called Christians. After this,
you request my ignorance to solve this problem.

This is your first question, the answer to which is difficult
for me for the many reasons which I have stated, but chiefly
because one who is buried in darkness cannot offer leadership
to one who sees.[5] Now, since you ask me to give you my
opinion, ask the person who is said to be subject to a malediction whether, at the time the malediction was spoken and
in the presence of the bishop, he performed the office of
priest and was not forbidden by him; whether he baptized,
anointed with chrism, celebrated mass, and was allowed to do
so by the one who was aware of having pronounced the malediction. It seems to me that not the priest, but the one who
did one thing by deceit and pretended to be doing another
is to blame. Therefore, the one whose act was so sinful will,
it seems to me, "bear his own burden,"[6] while your holiness

---

5 Cf. Matt. 15.14.
6 Gal. 6.5.

will be immune from this crime, because you permit each one to remain in the calling in which you found him.[7] I do not see why he should not be considered a priest, if the bishop who did not want him to be a priest publicly recognized him to be a priest; nor why those anointed by him with holy unction should not be called Christians, for, even though he is unworthy, they still have been anointed with a true chrism.

Your prudence well knows that ancient canons have forbidden a priest to have the audacity to administer chrism, a prohibition observed up to now, as we know, in the Orient and throughout Italy; later, priests were permitted to administer chrism, provided the chrism was blessed by the bishops,[8] in order that it would not appear to be a privilege of priests to consecrate the people of God with this holy unction, but only of the bishops, by whose benediction and permission they perform the ministration, as if by the hand of a bishop. If this is so, why should they not be considered Catholics who were anointed by him, as if by the hand of a bishop, although an unworthy one, since, as I said, they were anointed with a holy and true chrism, blessed by the bishop, and with his permission? It is manifest that baptisms given in the name of the Trinity should not be repeated, but we are not forbidden to anoint with chrism heretics whom we find not to have shared the true chrism.[9] He anointed them with a true chrism, as I have said; it does not seem that what he has done is invalid.

There is the additional fact that he who permitted him to perform never contradicted him, and did not hesitate to entrust to him the chrism which he had blessed, and thereby himself performed what the other did. What difference does it make whether the act was performed under pretext or was authentic? Since it was performed in a Catholic church,

---

7 Cf. 1 Cor. 7.20.
8 The method of administering this rite was standardized for Spain by Canon 20 of the First Council of Toledo.
9 Cf. Isidore, *De eccl. off.* 2.25.9.

it must not be repeated. Those who report after the death of your predecessor that he told them these stories will do better if they save that matter for another life. Now that he is gone, who will be able to contradict them, or who will be able to correct their objections. What he did not disperse, you must not disperse, mindful of these words: "Pass no judgment before the time";[10] and again: "what is manifest, to us; what is secret, to God."[11]

To the best of my poor ignorance and small capacity, I have answered in full, without affirming or denying. Now, if you do not object, let us turn to the other question.

You also write that in some places you have found deacons offering chrism. In this question, as in the first, the only answer which I can give is that holy chrism remains under your authority and the indulgence of the bishop. Those who have offered it through ignorance or presumption must be placed under the penalty and penance of severe and proper sentence against them, in accordance with ecclesiastical laws, and they are to be so punished that they will become an example to others and never presume such things again.

Having set down these two questions in brief, I find that your prudence has proposed to my ignorance a third, namely, that some priests presume to anoint the baptized with chrism which they make themselves, if that is to be called chrism. I must say that you have reason to be hesitant, for that is not chrism which appears to have been consecrated, not only not by bishops, but against the established law and prohibitions of the canons. For if the heavenly Master and Lord left His vicariate to His bishops, then, what was constituted by them was constituted by the spirit of Christ,[12] according to the apostle, and if anyone spurns their precepts, he spurns the precepts of Christ. Therefore, it seems to me that those who have been fraudulently anointed by such should again be

10 1 Cor. 4.5.
11 Deut. 29.29.
12 Cf. Acts 20.28.

anointed with the holy and true chrism. The punishment of the presumptuous is left to your judgment, however, for it is one thing to correct a mistake, something else to condemn one who is presumptuous. It is part of your wisdom to deal more kindly with the ignorant and to punish the presumptuous severely.

Impeded as I am by an unlearned tongue, I had hoped to produce a short letter, but, as runs the expression well known to you, "While I strive to make a pitcher, my hands have produced a jar."[13]

Now I pay my respects and commend to your prayers the comforting of my daily troubles and continuous tribulations, and I beseech you through Christ that whatever you find spread on these pages that is impractical or contrary to reason shall not be made public until you have written again to inform me. I had not time enough to think nor sufficient leisure for dictation; I have used the hand of another to put down what my tongue brought forth; I had no opportunity to read it over.

LETTER 37

A petition

Braulio and Eutropius, your bishops and servants, with the priests, deacons, and all the people entrusted to them by God, also your servant Celsus with the territories entrusted to him by your clemency, to our most glorious lord, King Chindaswinth.[1]

He who holds the hearts of kings in His hands, as we believe, also rules everything. Hence, it is by His inspiration

---

13 Cf. *Letters* 11 and 44.

1 This letter of 35 lines is essentially one continuous sentence in the Latin. Braulio is here associated with Eutropius, probably the one who received *Letter* 22, and Celsus, probably a governor or count of the region around Saragossa. They are suggesting to King Chinda-

that we desire to make petition to your clemency. Therefore, pious lord, gladly receive the prayers of your servants, which you behold inspired by the intention of faith. We have conferred with one another in hope and with that frequent devotion to thought by which each one seeks tranquillity of life and avoids disasters; we have considered past crises; we have noticed to what dangers, to what troubles, to what incursions of our enemies we are exposed; as we contemplate seriously what you have been protected from by heavenly mercy and what we have been saved from by your rule, we think of your labors as we look towards the future of our country; we are vacillating between hope and fear, but hope conquers fear, and so we have decided to have recourse to your piety to ask you to make your servant, Lord Receswinth, our lord and king while you are still alive and in good health, for we see no more convenient way to suit your repose and our difficulties. He is still of the age to wage war and suffer the sweat of battles, he is aided by grace from above, and can be our lord and defender and the comfort of your serene highness to settle the incursions and riots of the enemy and to make the life of your faithful subjects secure and free from terror. It will not be to your glorious credit to scorn such a son, and advancement is owed to the son of such a father.

Hence we pray with humble entreaty to the King of Heaven and the Ruler of all thrones, who set up Jesus [i.e., Josue][2] as successor to Moses, and placed on David's throne his son, Solomon,[3] that He with clemency plant in your minds the suggestion which we have presented, and that He accomplish with the aid of His Omnipotence what we in His name hope to receive from you. Though we may incur the charge of

---

swinth, who is now an octogenarian, that he should confer some of the royal power upon his son, Receswinth, while designating him successor. Since this conferral of authority was actually accomplished on Jan. 21, 649, the letter must have been written in 648.

2 Cf. Jos. 1.1-9.
3 Cf. 3 Kings 2.12.

rashness in our petition, we do not act from insolence of presumption, for as we have already said, we have thought this through carefully.

LETTER 38

Braulio, unworthy servant of the saints of God and your servant, to our glorious lord, King Receswinth.[1]

Although postponing one's promises is a form of lying, I wish to state the reason for my tardiness. The deplorable state of the book which I have received for correction has mustered all its forces against my clouded vision, and while I try to conquer them, the very vision which was becoming blind seemed to aid the enemy and to multiply obscurity to its own detriment. It will be apparent to your glory, however, how much labor there is in it, how exacting it is, how many times I have despaired of correcting it, and how many times I have given it up because of various ailments that interfered, only to return again to the interrupted task[2] with the intention of fulfilling your request, adding a line here and deleting letters there; for it is so cluttered up with scribal negligences that I find hardly a sentence which does not need correction, and hence it would have been quicker to rewrite the whole thing than it is to correct it already written. At the command of your serene highness, however, we desire ardently to give recognition to the welfare of your kingdom with all our prayers and ask Almighty God that your clemency's good fortunes may be increased.

---

1 The next four letters were written during the last three years of Braulio's life, 649-651. They concern a manuscript which Braulio is emending and rearranging for the king. A recent theory holds that this manuscript was the start of the famous Visigothic code of laws, *Forum Iudicum*, adopted in finished form in 654. Cf. Lynch, *op. cit.* 135-40, for a full discussion and strong support of this theory.

2 Cf. Jerome, *Letter* 125.12 (CSEL 56.131).

LETTER 39

His excellency to the holy and venerable father, Bishop Braulio.[1]

Our clemency has joyfully received and unsealed your sanctity's graceful letter in which you note, not without some complaint, the difficulty of your task of emending the book which our highness recently sent you. As you state that your eyesight is being dimmed by the great frequency of the errors which you find in it, we are compassionate for the holy ardor which you distill, but we are in part refreshed by the thought that while you write, your holiness is unfurling the sails of his vigilance and with favorable breezes flying by divine grace to the task of removing or correcting the errors of the scribes. The courage of your strength and the copious foresight of inner vision will be granted you by the Lord in answer to your prayers as your incisive intellect constantly strives to delete the corruptions and faults of the copyists; our glory will be made more happy and will exult when your paternity, as we expect, has fulfilled its promises with achievements.

Finally, we are well, as God has granted us to be, and we are always delighted to learn that your beatitude is well.

LETTER 40

Braulio, unworthy servant of the saints of God and your servant, to our glorious lord, King Receswinth.[1]

In trying to satisfy the command of your highness, I have laid bare the secrets of my ignorance and, as you bade, have

---

1 Written 649-651 as an answer to *Letter* 38.

1 Written 649-651, after completion of the corrections to the manuscript mentioned in the two preceding letters.

arranged the text of this book by subject matter and titles.
Would that my success equalled my obedience! If there is
anything displeasing, the inadequacy of my intelligence has
done it; but if there is anything pleasing, as I rather hope, the
gift will be His who revealed the laziness of the ass through
the measures of human speech.[2] I beseech your piety, most
serene prince, that you do not reckon my inability on this
score, for although I could not do as well as I wanted, I did
use effort. If any of the material which I have collected seems
imperfect to any of your servants, let them not hesitate to refer
to the chapter from which it was gathered. As for what
remains . . . [3]

LETTER 41

*Our highness to the saint and venerable father, Bishop
Braulio.*[1]

We have received the communication of your beatitude in
which in regard to this book that our serene highness had
given your holiness to be corrected, you reveal in all nakedness
the ignorance which had been hidden. It is the custom of a
wise man to judge himself ignorant, lest he become elated
and inclined to boast, but since the inspiration of divine
virtue "blows where it will"[2] upon everyone, you are most
deserving that we praise this work which you have completed, because, in this book, you instantly displayed your
obedience and, as I wished, you have wisely gathered its
efficacy and made it accessible, for which we render thanks
to your paternity, though insufficiently, and, in addition,
we return the greeting and ask that you deign to pray for us.

---

2 Cf. Num. 22.28-30.
3 The end of this letter is missing in the manuscript.

---

1 An answer to *Letter* 40, written 649-651.
2 Cf. John 3.8 and *Letter* 32 n. 3.

FRAGMENT OF A LETTER
FROM ABBOT TAJO TO BISHOP BRAULIO[1]

... Such a religion is pious, to be sure, but to me it is questionable. Therefore, most holy of men, I bring this sort of query to your ears, and if it is definitely to be believed, as I have already said, that the Blood of the Lord remained with certain individuals after His Resurrection, I want to be informed by you with unimpeachable testimony and the surest proofs. I should like to receive a treatise on this matter from your generosity. The Lord Jesus Christ will furnish me a sure proof without ambiguity, if my prayers are fulfilled by you.

Finally, with all the humility which I possess, I presume to greet the sanctity of my lord, beseeching that I may deserve to be commended in your prayers and to be informed as soon as possible by a letter from you on the matter which I have discussed.

LETTER 42

Braulio, worthless servant of servants, to the venerable Tajo, priest and abbot, most revered in the members of Christ and brother in Christ.[1]

I confess that I have been restrained by various difficulties from answering your letter immediately, but more especially

---

1 Written in 649 or 650 after Tajo's return from a lengthy stay in Rome. The part preserved is only the end of a longer letter in which Tajo posed the question: "Since some churches possess supposed relics of our Lord's blood, does this mean that our Lord's risen body did not reassume His blood, and that we shall not reassume ours after resurrection?" This much is clear from Braulio's reply in *Letter* 42. Lynch has assumed that Tajo, as Braulio's successor to the See of Saragossa, was the editor of the whole collection of Braulio's correspondence, but even so I can see no sensible reason for a deletion by Tajo. There are other not very large gaps in the text tradition; why not one here also?

---

1 Written in 649 or 650 in reply to the fragmentary letter just preceding.

by trouble with my eyes and by the affliction of several infirmities. Now that I have a chance to breathe amid my troubles, I have hastened to read your letter again and I there find that your goodness hopes for a good many things from me which I know that I can certainly not fulfill.

What can there be in me, even to a small degree, that you expect from me the imitation of so many and such great men? You read them constantly yourself as befits your age, you are always searching them for knowledge, and their words are, if I may use the phrase, nested in your heart.[2] Leisure is a blessed possession for you, but a burden to me amid the waves of my present life; I am like a seagoing bark that is not much used or is plagued with bilge water or lying damaged. Even though the things you seek from me were unworthily conferred upon me by the generosity of nature, they would never be presumed by me, "for you know that my attitude is to wave the flag of humility" and to prefer to rest on a strong, level surface rather than to climb to the heights up steps that ascend dangerously.[3] Therefore, I beg you, my dearest friend, to make less complaint of the weaknesses and desires of those who live around you, since you should bear all things patiently. What harm can another's compliance with evil do to those who are virtuous? "It is not especially praiseworthy to be good with the good, but rather to be good with the bad."[4]

It is written of the Church: "As a lily among thorns, so is my beloved among women."[5] Those who are believed by us to be such probably need only, as the apostle puts it, "to know Christ, and him crucified."[6] He Himself teaches us: "Not setting your mind on high things, but condescending to the

---

2 The five books of *Sententiae* by Tajo, published in PL 80.727-990, are composed mostly of extensive quotations from works of St. Gregory the Great with many excerpts from St. Augustine.
3 Jerome, *Letter* 47.1 (CSEL 54.345).
4 Gregory, *Moralia* 1.1 (PL 75.529).
5 Cant. 2.2.
6 Cf. 1 Cor. 2.2.

lowly"; and "Be not wise in your own conceits";[7] "Knowledge
puffs up, but charity edifies";[8] and other things which cannot
be unknown to you. In this sense is Catholic humility possessed, and the words, "Let every man be convinced in his
own mind,"[9] are no doubt fulfilled. Hence, the same apostle
preached that "we should not please ourselves, but our
neighbors."[10] He writes to the Philippians that "in humility
we regard the others as our superiors";[11] "each one looking
not to his own interests but to those of others";[12] "that man
may not glory in his prudence,"[13] for the virtue of the humble
is not to boast of their knowledge, since it is common to all.
In repressing the mind's audacity, it is very helpful not to
despise others, nor to assume a special knowledge or holiness
ourselves, lest we hear in the words of the divine oracle:
"I have left for myself seven thousand men [who have not
bowed the knee to Baal.]"[14]

Your charity must believe, I beg, that I have said this because I love you. As to the question on which you decided
to consult me, you must know that, concerning the resurrection
of the dead, I do not believe or expect otherwise than what
has been expressed with prudent thought and elegant language
by St. Augustine in several of his works, which I have not
sought out because I wanted to save myself the trouble and
because I learned from your letter that you clearly have them
yourself.[15]

---

7 Cf. Rom. 12.16.
8 1 Cor. 8.1.
9 Rom. 14.5.
10 Cf. Rom. 15.1, 2.
11 Cf. Phil. 2.3.
12 Cf. Phil. 2.4.
13 Cf. Jer. 9.23.
14 Rom. 11.4. The here bracketed completion of the verse is represented
   in the edition by "et cetera."
15 Although the references are purposely not made specific, Madoz suggests as sources for the present discussion: Augustine, *Enchiridion*
   23 and 84-92; *De trin.* 4.3; *De civ. Dei* 22.12-19; the latter was certainly
   in Braulio's library, as the book is mentioned by name below.

Therefore, I do not doubt that in the resurrection our blood is to be reassumed, though I doubt that the blood that we receive over the entire course of our lives will be completely restored in its own quality, because it is shown to be superfluous, not our own, according to the doctors, but harmful to us. If that beauty which the saints are going to have allows, I think it will happen; if it does not allow, then we must believe here the same as you have learned from the words of St. Augustine in regard to superfluous nail parings and hair, which, in the intermingling of nature, shall be restored to other parts of the members. It lies within the skill of the omnipotence of our Creator to diminish the large and to increase the small as He wills, but it must be believed that in the resurrection nothing restored to the members of the saints will be without beauty.

Therefore, I believe that the Lord remembers and includes the smallest and most remote of our limbs when He speaks of the hair;[16] but if the hair does not perish, how much less shall greater parts perish?[17] But the superfluous fluids, by which corruptions are born or vices generated, I do not believe are included, for they, certainly, will not exist in the resurrected body.

I believe that everything which pertains to our own nature will be restored in the resurrection, for everything in nature that has come into existence unnecessarily or that has corrupted nature or has been able to transform its appearance must be removed. Now, by "nature," I have intended that in accordance with which the body of man is constituted whole and sound. So, since we cannot be without blood, in which the virtue of the soul is placed in the body by divine authority,[18] it must be restored to us, not superfluous but natural, that is, not another's but our own.

---

16 Cf. Luke 21.18.
17 Augustine *De civ. Dei* 22.20.2.
18 Cf. Lev. 17.14.

In short, I can believe this and it is not difficult to affirm, but it is clear that there should be even less doubt that each one will properly receive at the resurrection, with corruptions and vices removed, as I have said, that body, reasonably and wholly constituted, which he could have had at that time when the Lord suffered; in the words of the apostle: "Have this mind in you which was also in Christ Jesus";[19] and elsewhere: "Until we all meet to perfect manhood to the mature measure of the fullness of Christ."[20]

We should, however, be cautious in this inquiry, for the chosen vessel reproves: "Let no one rate himself more than he ought, but let him rate . . . according to moderation,"[21] lest we go so far as to be found superstitious: like those who put questions about aborted fetuses which have their corporeal substance from the two sexes: what could be held about the menstrual blood and also the impure fluid which in nearly every life must be discharged naturally, matters in which their superstition will be excessive.

Why should it not be believed that human blood is drawn off and perishes, when the fluid of generation and the blood, as well as the miscarriage, are not restored in the resurrection to either parent, if such a one can indeed be termed a parent, who loses the abominable fluid or a lifeless fetus? But there are some[22] who assure us that this is the true blood of Christ which a number of people hold as relics, as you say, and that His blood was not reassumed in the Resurrection of the body of the Lord, just as this blood was not reassumed. That is the reason for the column at Jerusalem, spattered with His blood, which was seen and described several centuries later by the remarkable priest, St. Jerome[23] and by others. This we should take as proof of the Divine Passion rather than to

---

19 Phil. 2.5.
20 Cf. Eph. 4.13.
21 Rom. 12.3.
22 Reading *nonnulli* for *non . . . hi.*
23 Jerome, *Letter* 108.9 (CSEL 55.315).

deny this proof of piety, since we have it described in the
writings of our ancestors.

It is possible that many things happened then which have
not been written down, just as we read of the linen cloths
and the shroud in which the body of Christ was wrapped,[24]
that they were found, yet we do not hear that they were preserved; yet I do not suppose that the apostles neglected to
save these and other such things for future times.

In this matter, however, we must not leave ourselves open
to the enemies of the Catholic Church, lest, by the poison of
falsehood or for the sake of malediction, they might wish to
seduce the chaste virgin of Christ. Or perhaps the most sacred
blood was scraped off from this column by the faithful and
scattered over the whole world to be used as relics, which I
could easily believe, so that it might be reported by the
leaders of the Church to their succeeding posterity that it had
been preserved, for I cannot see how the report of such an
important matter can be doubtful to Christians.

There is still more to say on this matter: perhaps the
sweat of the Lord, which the Gospel tells us flowed like
blood,[25] may be supposed to have been collected by His disciples with proper diligence; or, certainly, when the body
of the Lord was struck with the lance and blood and water
flowed,[26] it was, through someone's care, preserved for relics,
but I really wonder if this can be proved by anyone, since
the doubt and hesitation of the disciples even at the Passion
can later be discovered;[27] and John stood alone with the
women by the Lord's Cross, yet, when he wrote his Gospel,
he never mentioned that he or anyone else had done such a
thing;[28] he offered witness and wrote down the true witness,
that the body of the Lord was struck down with the lance and

---

24 Cf. John 20.5-7.
25 Cf. Luke 22.44.
26 Cf. John 19.34.
27 Cf. Matt. 28.17.
28 Cf. John 20; Luke 24.10.

that the blood and water flowed out,[29] but he never mentions that it was collected by anyone.

Now if, in the place where he writes: "There are many other-signs which Jesus made which are not written in this book,"[30] someone construes this to mean that he spoke about this blood, let him prove, if possible, that this is a sign, but he will find it difficult to persuade me. If it is not affirmed by the authority of Scripture, then, as you say, belief may be pious but nods uncertainly, since the Bridegroom of Verity has regard, not only for what is truly pious, but also for what is piously true, and truth is firm when the piously true does not nod. Let him affirm this who is able; I can only confess my ignorance in the matter.

Now then, we may give up these thoughts and leave them in the power of the reader, since they are by no means prejudicial to our faith in the Resurrection. We ought not to forbid a more minute investigation, nor oppose the authority of the multitude, which asserts that relics of this kind are to be found in cathedral churches, although they have never been found in my church in the time of any bishop. It is better to be in doubt about hidden matters than to quarrel about what is uncertain. Let us turn to what is true and firm, to what most assuredly keeps any Christian and good Catholic from doubting or quibbling: namely, that through the sacrament bread and wine offered to God become for us the true Body and Blood of Christ, according to the words of the Lord Himself and the Sacred Scriptures composed by the Holy Spirit, which sacrament the Catholic Church offers daily on her altar "according to the order of Melchisedech"[31] by the true Pontiff, Jesus Christ, with mystical understanding and an ineffable dearth of speech, because surpassing grace goes beyond everything.

---

29 Cf. John 19.34.
30 Cf. John 21.25.
31 Heb. 7.17.

It must be enough, my dearest friend, for me to have answered you briefly, as the thoughts came to me and as the time allowed; although I may not have answered sufficiently to match your immense eagerness, still, I tried to comply with your desires, as my leisure permitted. Finally, I must earnestly request to be favored in your beatitude's prayers.

There is one thing which is necessary for me above all others and I had forgotten to mention it; if you grant it, may Christ make the course of your life glorious. Please send me quickly to be copied the books of the holy Pope Gregory which previously did not exist in Spain, but which have been brought here from Rome by your zeal and effort;[32] for I am not the only petitioner in this matter, but also, my lord and brother, your friend.[33] Therefore, you satisfy both if you do one a favor, and you hurt both if you spurn one. Your charity must believe that I will return the books at any time set by you.

I had thought I was producing a short letter,[34] but spurred on as I was in various directions by whispered anxieties, I was neither able to remain brief nor to say everything that was troubling me. Farewell in the Lord, dearest brother, worthy to be embraced with reverence in the members of Christ.

---

[32] Tajo's journey to Rome may have been solely to get copies of the later works of Gregory the Great. It is known that Isidore had previously used Gregory's *Liber regulae pastoralis*, the first edition of the *Moralia*, and some letters. Any of the other works of Gregory may have been located by Tajo, but it is not possible to identify them with certainty. Ildefonse, who extended Isidore's *De viris illustribus* a few years later, added the names of Gregory's *Dialogues, Commentary on the Canticle of Canticles*, and 22 *Homilies on Ezekiel.*

[33] Fronimian, to whom the *Life of Emilian* was dedicated.

[34] Cf. Jerome, *Letter* 104.6 (CSEL 55.242).

LETTER 43

Fructuosus, insignificant and always your servant, to my own lord, Bishop Braulio.[1]

We have learned from the story in Sacred Scripture how pleasing to a man is "good news from a far country";[2] and what other better news could we expect than the love of Christ, than the spotless profession and propagation of the Catholic Church, than the pure lives, successful work, and faithful doctrine of the friends of God and the bishops and priests of Christ? These, most blessed father, we confess that we vehemently yearn for and thirstingly desire to learn.

This news alone often sustains the dried vital parts of our mind, and in view of the success of your deeds amid the raucous breakers of the spuming salt waves and the whirlpools of the ocean and the restless seas, our humble ears are soothed by the news that your constant sublime teaching ennobles your Saragossa, and that the life of your eminence, flowering each day, abounds with zeal for the divine law and is to an equal extent fortified by the constant and sedulous preaching of your good works.

Therefore, unceasingly we give praise to our King and Creator, the Lord, that, with the end of the world now approaching, you, so great a bishop, exist, who, endowed with merit of life and richness of doctrine, follow in all the steps of the apostles, pursuing their stainless life in this stormy world and soon to receive with them the ineffable glory of the supernal fatherland. Undertaking a bold task, perhaps, I presume to salute your most pious sanctity and, in one and the same message, we pray that we may be refreshed with news of your health and with specimens of your sacred writings. Begging, I ask for the leftover bits of crumbs from the ban-

---

1 Written from somewhere in northwestern Spain, before Fructuosus became Bishop of Braga and not long before Braulio's death in 651.
2 Prov. 25.25.

quets of your tables,[3] and from a spiritual father, abounding
in the treasures of heavenly wisdom, I seek a gift of some
small talent; that I may receive it, I keep the watches of the
night like an importunate petitioner. Although negligent,
yet seeking, I ask and knock.[4] Relying on the aid of the
saints of God, whose solace we enjoy, I beg that you lay open
to your unworthy and most worthless friend what I do not
know and grant what I do not have.

First of all then, I demand that my lord, filled with the
teaching of the early fathers and the doctrine of the Holy
Spirit, deign to explain, in a brief and clearly stated page or
two to me, your leprous friend and to the ulcerous novice,
Eleazer,[5] certain problems which Jerome, the father of sanctity
and sharer of your glory, a most blessed and most learned
man, failed to clarify. And if you do so, may the Lord open
to you the entrance to His heavenly kingdom.

Given that the aforementioned scholar says that Mathusale
lived fourteen years after the flood, and if all the flesh which
was not in the ark perished in the cataclysm, the question is:
where was he that he escaped, since we do not read that he
entered the ark with the others? He added of Agar that, while
fleeing her mistress, she carried on her back Ismael, who was
a full-grown young man. I want to know how that is explained.
Then, he brought up a similar question in his passage about
Solomon; if one deducts the periods of time mentioned
and notes the years that have passed, it is discovered that,
according to the text of the Scripture, Solomon was in his
eleventh year when he begat his son Roboam. This is hardly
possible.[6]

---

3 Cf. Luke 16.21.
4 Cf. Luke 11.5-9; Matt. 7.7, 8.
5 Eleazer for Lazarus; cf. Luke 16.20.
6 These three questions are posed in almost identical language by
  Jerome, *Letter to Damasus*, 36.10 (CSEL 54.276-77). Fructuosus must
  have possessed the *Letters* of Jerome, but not the *Hebrew Questions*,
  from which Braulio quotes at length in his reply.

The request that this matter be explained to me and my fellow captives is not made with any cleverness of fluent speech, as some are accustomed to do, but with pure and sincere affection and love for you and with genuine desire to learn the truth.

I am especially suppliant, my lord, that you enlighten our monasteries by your generosity with the *Conferences* of Cassian,[7] which cannot be found in this whole area in which we live, though we have searched. We also request that out of your bounty you make a present to us, unworthy though we are, of the *Lives* of the holy men Honoratus[8] and Germanus,[9] and your beatitude's own recent *Life of Emilian*.[10] You regularly fill the wants of others with the honey of your eloquence; do not refuse to do the same for us, so far remote and sunk low in the obscure lands of the west. Do this, most pious lord, that your reward may shine before God.

We already have here, thanks to certain Christians, the seven *Conferences* of the aforementioned Cassian, which he wrote to Jovinian, Minervius, Leontius, and Theodore, but the next ten *Conferences,* which he says he published for the bishops Helladius and Leontius, and the final seven, which he says he published for Saints Honoratus and Eucherius, we do not have. We ask that we may deserve to receive them from your bounty.

Farewell in the 'Lord and remember us, blessed father. Your humble servants, all the poor who are with us, salute

---

7 The *Conlationes* or *Conferences* of St. John Cassian in 24 books are so long that they have survived today in the same threefold tradition which Fructuosus mentions below, I-VII, VIII-XVII, XVIII-XXIV. The best edition is that of M. Petschenig, CSEL 13 (Vienna 1886). The *prologomena* describing the manuscript tradition are found in CSEL 17 (Vienna 1888).

8 The *Life of St. Honoratus of Arles* is preserved as a sermon by St. Hilary of Arles (PL 50.1249-72); new English version in F. R. Hoare, *The Western Fathers* (New York 1954) 247-80.

9 The *Life of St. Germanus, Bishop of Auxerre* by Constance of Lyon is found in MGH, *scr. mer.* 7 (1929) 225-83, ed. W. Levison; translated by Hoare, *op. cit.* 283-320.

10 Translated in this volume pp. 113-39.

your holiness most earnestly and ask that you do not refuse the request of your abject servant, but assist the prayers of a suppliant; may the saints of God remember your worthiness.

LETTER 44

Braulio, unworthy servant of the saints of God, to my lord, deservedly outstanding, most sweet son in the members of Christ, Fructuosus the priest.[1]

Between the declaration of your praises of me and the merits of my own deeds, I must preside as an unprejudiced arbiter using reasonable arguments, and I must believe, under a true and severe judgment, that I am what I feel myself to be from within and not what I hear on the outside from others who think otherwise. Generally, it is solely from a feeling of good will that "the good man from the good treasure of his heart brings forth good things;"[2] surely, a fresh spring will not be able to produce salty water. Again, it generally happens that human opinions are deceived, and that the evil is judged good and the good evil. It is not so much this thought which must be feared: "Woe to those who call evil good, and good evil,"[3] if one is deceived by love or at least out of his own goodness judges[4] an evil man good; but rather must we avoid those persons in whom vices please rather than virtues, or at any rate virtues displease rather than vices, so that, following this erroneous law, they either think an evil man good or a good man evil. He who calls a man good, because he thinks him to be just and does not know that he is unjust, is deceived, not in his understanding of good and evil things, but in the secret ways of human character.

---

1 Written in 651 as an answer to *Letter* 43.
2 Cf. Matt. 12.35; the word *cordis* is not in the Vulgate, but is found in Jerome's quotation of this same verse in *Letter* 65.5 (CSEL 54.622).
3 Cf. Isa. 5.20 and quotation in Jerome, *Letter* 62.2 (CSEL 54.584).
4 Reading *aestimet* for *timet*.

I know myself and you must realize the truth of my claim that I am not such as you describe me. This I may properly say to you, whom I hold in Christ in the members of Christ and for the grace of Christ. But our conduct of life must not, by any means, be revealed to those of whom it is said: "Let not the oil of the sinner fatten my head,"[5] those for whom this very adulation of oil shall in the end fail among the foolish and stupid virgins.[6] For of what avail is it to reveal oneself to one from whom you cannot receive a remedy for your faults? Accordingly, we should confess our faults to those by whose prayers we may receive aid or provide examples of good conduct. "The just man shall correct me in mercy," he said, and "shall reprove me."[7] And of these it is said: "Confess your sins to one another, and pray for one another."[8] Since it would be a long and unpleasant task to reveal my sinful ways to you and to tell you all in order, it must be sufficient to reveal to your most holy mind that I am not what you believe, though I beg you to pray that God make me such as you believe.

Now that I have forbidden you to do this, I shall turn to praise of you, and you are doubtless going to say: "Why do you do yourself what you forbid?" I must necessarily favor my side while I pay you my debt, for we are instructed by the apostle to "render to all men whatever is their due"[9] and to "owe no man anything."[10] Surely, I am not deceived about my own worth, but, for your modesty's sake, I forbear to speak of how worthy you seem to me; would that you had preserved this modesty by saying less in praise of me.

I must praise your soul, but in the Lord, in whom we should praise the upright; whence the psalmist says: "Praise

---

5 Cf. Ps. 140.5.
6 Cf. Matt. 25.1-13.
7 Cf. Ps. 140.5.
8 James 5.16.
9 Rom. 13.7.
10 Rom. 13.8.

from the upright is fitting";[11] and "In the Lord shall my
soul be glorified,"[12] to whom belongs and from whom comes
every good thing,[13] to whom we offer thanks for your efforts
and progress. The more I realize the faith you show in speaking of me, the more it feels right for me to be heavily oppressed; it is thus that you must receive what I am eager
to say.

How happy you are for having abandoned the business of
this world and chosen in advance the holy leisure! I understand, love, cherish, and embrace the ardor and vigor of your
mind, the brightness of the light that shines in the Holy Spirit;
I pant with thirsty longing that your merits may prevail before
God for my sins and crimes. How blessed is that desert and
vast solitude which recently knew only wild beasts and is now
filled with the habitations of monks, congregated by you
and singing praises of God; of pilgrims of the world, citizens
of God, captives from Babylon, predestined to Jerusalem.
I praise and extol in Christ you and yours, whose zeal adorns
a desert far different from the desert which Jerome[14] and
Eucherius,[15] most learned and outstanding men, once beauti-
fied with the charming flowers of their words and sentiments.
To compress much into a short space and, as it were, to paint
the world on a small tablet,[16] since I have no time to proceed
at length, nor the keenness of talent nor the eloquence of
tongue, I shall change for your benefit the ancient praise of a
gentile poet and shall say only: O sacred glory of Spain![17]
Do not believe that I am performing the office of a flatterer
of vices or of one who adulates, but I cannot keep silent
concerning what I believe about you, since my ministry is to

11 Ps. 32.1.
12 Cf. Ps. 33.3.
13 Cf. Heb. 2.10.
14 Jerome, *Letter* 14 (CSEL 54.44-62) and elsewhere.
15 Eucherius, *In Praise of the Desert* (CSEL 31.175-94).
16 This phrase or a similar one is found in several of Jerome's *Letters*.
17 Madoz may be right in thinking "O decus Hispaniae sacrum" an
   adaptation of "O decus Italiae virgo," Vergil, *Aeneid* 11.508. No better
   identification of the "gentile poet" has been suggested.

speak the truth. So great is it that, by your perseverance,
things have been brought to an end "by patience" in which
we are bidden to "win our souls";[18] for "whoever perseveres
to the end, he shall be saved."[19] "Now the purpose of this
charge is charity,"[20] which, according to John "is God";[21]
and God is Christ, "for whom are all things,"[22] and we should
not act for any other cause; in this, the psalmist sees the "end
of all perfection,"[23] which is the reason why the titles of some
Psalms are headed by "unto the end."[24] For those who come
to this end there will be no further place to which the course
of the faithful may be directed, in the words of Him who
said: "Come to me, all you who labor and are burdened, and
I will give you rest."[25] May your zeal continue to burn as it
has begun, and send greater flames in the Lord, for it will
fall back if it does not proceed just as a skiff on a very rapid
current of water slips down to lower levels if it does not constantly progress higher.

In your section of the country, be on your guard, even at
this late date, against the poisonous dogma of Priscillianism,
by which we know Dictinius was infected as well as many
others, including St. Orosius, who was later set aright by St.
Augustine. To such an extent has Priscillian distorted the
Scriptures by the zeal of his heresy that even to this day we
find many books depraved by the taint of this corruptor.[26]

---

18 Luke 21.19.
19 Matt. 24.13.
20 1 Tim. 1.5.
21 1 John 4.16.
22 Heb. 2.10.
23 Ps. 118.96.
24 Isidore in the *Praef.* to the Psalter says that the Septuagint has titles
"psalm unto the end" where the Hebrew has "to Victor."
25 Matt. 11.28.
26 The middle of the seventh century is very late for a warning against
the adherents of Priscillianism. Braulio seems rather to be worried
about the numerous Bible texts still in existence containing heretical
passages. Dictinius of Astorga was the strongest of the followers of
Priscillian, until he renounced that heresy in 400. Orosius was a not-

Do not be led astray by popular favor or the vanity of vainglory, for this is the last struggle among the athletes of God, in whom is the final judgment.[27] Now, not to protract my letter unduly, I shall come to the questions which you proposed and, as you hoped, I shall quote the opinions of our ancestors, such as I have read and as they occur to me; certain matters, for the sake of brevity, I shall put together in my own words.

This is the beginning of your petition: "First of all," you say, "I demand that you explain to me in a brief and clearly stated passage or two from your reading of the early fathers certain problems which Jerome, the father of sanctity and sharer of your glory, the most blessed and most learned of men, failed to clarify." I have no idea why you say this, since that most holy man left a clear exposition of the matter in his book called *Hebrew Questions*.[28] This is the solution which he offers: "There is a famous question which has been aired by discussion in all churches: that, by a careful reckoning, it can be shown that Mathusale lived 14 years after the flood. When Mathusale was 167 years old, he became the father of Lamech; again, when Lamech was 188 years old, he became the father of Noe, and together they make 355 years of the life of Mathusale until the day of Noe's birth. Now the flood took place in the 600th year of Noe's life; so, by reckoning the separate parts it may be proved that the flood took place in the 955th year of Mathusale, but since it has been said above that Mathusale lived 969 years, no one can doubt that he lived 14 years after the flood. How can that be true,

---

able opponent of Priscillian's opinions, but this passage contains the only statement that he had been converted to this view by Augustine.

27 Cassian, *Inst.* 5.1 and 5.19 tit.

28 St. Jerome's *Hebrew Questions on Genesis* contain a critical examination of many passages where difficulties in the Old Latin version can be solved by reference to Hebrew and Greek texts. The present long quotation is from the commentary on Gen. 5.25-29 (*Corpus Christianorum: Series latina* 72.8-9; PL 23.946-47).

when only eight souls were saved in the ark?" So far the proposition; now the solution.

"It appears that, in this case as in many others, there is an error in the numbers. Among the Hebrews and the books of the Samaritans, I have found the text written thus: 'Mathusale lived 187 years and begot Lamech. Mathusale lived 782 years after he begot Lamech, and begot sons and daughters. And all the days of Mathusale were 969 years, and he died. And Lamech lived 182 years and begot Noe.'[29] Accordingly, there are 369 years from the day of Mathusale's birth to the day of Noe's birth; to these add Noe's 600 years, since the flood occurred in the 600th year of his life, and so it works out that Mathusale died in the 969th year of his life, in the same year when the flood began." If you would believe the truth of this with greater certainty, refer to the translation by this most holy of men and you will have no doubt.

St. Augustine also, in the fifteenth book *On the City of God,* while examining the difference in years between the Hebrew copies and the Septuagint, affirms the translation from the Hebrew and at the end of his discussion of the same matter[30] says among other things: "All the years of the life of Mathusale are reckoned at 969." A little later: "Subtracting 955 from the birth of Mathusale to the flood, there remain 14 years, the length of time he is supposed to have lived after the flood. Wherefore some say that, although he was not on earth, where it is clear that all nature was destroyed except what nature allows to survive in water, he spent some time with his father, who had been translated, and they believe he lived there until the flood passed, because they are unwilling to question the faith of the copies of the text"—of the Septuagint version, that is—"which the Church has accepted

29 Cf. Gen. 5.25-28.
30 These quotations are all from chapters 11 and 13 of Book XV of the *City of God.*

as the more trustworthy authority, and because they supposed that the copies owned by the Jews rather than their own do not have the truth. They do not admit that there is more likely to be a mistake on the part of the translators rather than that there is an error in that language from which the Scripture itself was translated into our tongue through the Greek." And after some other things: "This is an opinion or a mere suspicion each one may interpret as he pleases; it is certain, however, that Mathusale did not live after the flood, but died in the same year."

Then, after some intervening discussion of matters which are here omitted, he says: "One could more easily believe that when these copies were first made from Ptolemy's library, something of this sort may have occurred in a single copy, but the very first one made, from which it was widely spread and to which there might have been added a scribe's error: it is not absurd to suspect something like this in the question about the life of Mathusale." Then, not far along: "So this disagreement of numbers reported differently in Greek and Latin copies on the one hand and the Hebrew on the other might," he adds, "be attributed to the error of the scribe who first received the transcribed text to be copied from the library of the above-mentioned king."

Then, after a little while: "But however this is understood, whether or not it is believed that it happened this way, whether in the end it is one way and not the other, I should not hesitate to say that, when some difference is found in both sets of copies, inasmuch as the truth of what happened cannot be possessed by both sides, the right course is to believe that language from which the translation was made into another by interpreters. In some copies which agree, including three Greek, one Latin, and one Syrian, Mathusale is found to have died six years before the flood."

These matters St. Augustine sets down in various places, just as we have quoted them and just as the blessed Jerome recounts them, and we must not disagree with what these most learned men have thought.

Furthermore, Eucherius, a man of outstanding knowledge and remarkable intelligence, quite copious in words and thoughts and abundant in eloquence, mentions this problem in his surviving works as follows: "How is it that, by careful reckoning of the years of Mathusale, he is found to have lived 14 years after the flood, when only eight souls are reported to have been in the ark?" Answer: "There is an error in the number, since it is read in the books of the Hebrews that this number of 14 years was fulfilled before the flood."[31] These three writers seem enough for us to confirm this solution, since it is written: "In the testimony of two or three witnesses"[32] shall every word stand.

There are many who have written on these matters. In our own day Isidore, Bishop of Seville, incomparable man of learning, while trying to solve the origin of this name, says thus in his books of *Etymologies:* "Mathusale is glossed by: *He died,* which is evidently the etymology of the name. Some thought that he had been translated with his father and had outlived the flood. For this reason, *He died* was set down to signify that he did not live after the flood, but had died in the same cataclysm, since only eight men escaped the flood in the ark."[33]

Next, to your question about Ismael, that the mother [Agar] carried her son on her back; St. Jerome discusses it as follows in the book of *Questions* already mentioned:[34] " 'And Sara saw the son of Agar the Egyptian, whom she bore to Abraham, playing';[35] what follows, 'with her son Isaac,'

31 Eucherius, Bishop of Lyon, died about 450; cf. his *Two Books of Instructions to Salonius* 1.17, ed. Wotke (CSEL 31.71).
32 Deut. 17.6.
33 Book 7.6.13.
34 Commentary on Gen. 21.9-18 (*Corp. chr.: Ser. lat.* 72.24-25; PL 23.967-68) from which all the direct citations were taken, except the one noted. There are several variations from the Vulgate.
35 Gen. 21.9.

does not stand in the Hebrew. This is explained by the Hebrews in two ways: either that she made an idol of mud, as was
written elsewhere: 'The people sat down to eat and drink, and
rose up to revel';[36] or that she was, by sport and jest, establish-
ing her claim over the birthright against Isaac, who was the
elder. This Sara heard and could not endure. This is proved
by her own words when she said: 'Cast out this slave-girl with
her son; for the son of this slave-girl shall not be heir with my
son Isaac. And he took bread and a bottle of water, and gave to
Agar, placing her small son upon her shoulder, and dismissed
her.'[37] When Isaac was born, Ismael was 13 years old, and he
was cast out of the house with his mother after Isaac was
weaned. Among the Hebrews, there is a difference of opinion,
some claiming that the time of weaning is set in the fifth year,
others in the twelfth year. We for our part, choosing the
shorter time, have reckoned that Ismael was cast out with his
mother after 18 years and that it is not likely that an adolescent
sat on his mother's back. There is a genuine idiom of the
Hebrew language whereby every son by comparison with his
parents is called infant and small. Nor should we marvel at a
foreign language having its peculiarities when at Rome today
all sons are called infants. Therefore, Abraham set bread and a
bottle upon the shoulder of Agar, and when he had done so,
gave the boy to his mother, that is, put him in her hands,
entrusted him, and so sent them away from home.

"Next come the words: 'And she left the boy under a fir
tree, and she went and sat over against him a great way off
about the distance of a bowshot, for she said: "Let me not
see my child die"; and she sat over against him.'[38] And immediately is added: 'And the child cried aloud and wept and
God heard the boy's cry from the place where he was. And

---

36 Exod. 32.6.
37 Gen. 21.10, 14. The Latin here is uncertain (possibly a verb is missing), but it seems to say that Abraham placed the boy on Agar's
shoulder; Jerome's point, however, is that the Hebrew text states that
he placed the bread and water on her shoulder, not the boy.
38 Cf. Gen. 21.15-17.

the angel of God called to Agar from heaven,'[39] etc. This
should disturb no one, for in the Hebrew after the words:
'Let me not see my child die,' it is said that Agar herself sat
over against the boy and lifted her voice and wept and God
heard the voice of the boy. As the mother wept and wretchedly
awaited the death of her son, God heard the boy, of whom
He had made promise to Abraham, saying: 'But I will also
make the son of your slave-girl a great nation.'[40] For the
mother was weeping for her son's death, not her own. Therefore, God spared him for whom she had shed tears. Finally,
in the sequel, it is said: 'Rise up, take the boy, and hold him
by the hand,'[41] from which it is clear that he who was held
was not a burden to his mother, but a companion. That he
was held by the hand of his parent shows her anxious concern."

I admit that, on this matter, I have also read other interpreters of Scripture, but as it is naturally easy for me to forget,
I cannot recall in what work each one discussed the subject,
except those who have wished to allegorize, following the
apostle. To put it briefly, although some claim that the
Hebrews reckon the years to weaning sometimes as five,
sometimes as twelve, we have found a period of three years set
down for this same weaning in the Books of Machabees:
"My son," she said, "have pity upon me that bore thee nine
months in my womb and gave thee suck three years, and
brought thee up unto this age."[42] If one follows this authority,
two years should be removed from the sixteen. But when one
returns to the statement of divine Scripture, it is not found
in the Hebraic truth that Ismael was carried on the neck of
his mother. Why, then, cause so much trouble when we have
no difficulty?

Finally, on the question of Solomon, it remains for us to
call your attention to a passage about Solomon with which

39 Cf. Gen. 21.16, 17.
40 Cf. Gen. 21.18.
41 *Ibid.*
42 2 Mach. 7.27.

we know from your writings that you are already acquainted, since I understood, when reading the letter which you sent me, that you are familiar with a letter of the oft-mentioned blessed man Jerome to the priest Vitalis,[43] and what it contains about Solomon and Achaz and what he claims to have heard in his own day under the testimony of an oath. In the end of that letter, he shows a strong and sure belief in the omnipotence of God.

Nor can I think otherwise against the authority of so great a man, but I can only follow his steps and, in Christian humility, not deviate from the paths of our ancestors; as David says: "Neither have I walked with great things, nor with things too sublime for me."[44] He is raised up above himself who departs from the traces of his elders and tries to have vision in things which are beyond his powers. Hence, it follows: "If I was not humbly minded, but exalted my soul: as a child that is weaned is towards his mother, so wilt Thou reward in my soul."[45] And so it is useful for us to think humble thoughts, in the words of the apostle: "Not setting your mind on high things, but condescending to the lowly";[46] and to receive weaning with Isaac, that we may share stronger food rather than with Ismael, son of the slave-girl, to carry a bottle with water instead of wine[47] and to be driven from the eternal inheritance.

Having disposed of these matters in accordance with your wish, I report that I have not found any duplicates of the books which you ask to have me send to you. Of some, I have not even located single copies; I have discovered that they are missing from our shelves and I have been too busy to

---

43 Jerome, *Letter* 72 (CSEL 55.9-10) discusses the question whether it was possible for Solomon and Achaz to have sons when they were only eleven or twelve years old, but Fructuosus probably found the question posed without answer in *Letter* 36 (CSEL 54.276).
44 Cf. Ps. 130.1.
45 Cf. Ps. 130.2.
46 Cf. Rom. 12.16.
47 Cf. Gen. 21.9-18 and nn. 35, 37-41 above; Jerome, *Letter* 72.2 (CSEL 55.9-10).

institute a search, but if God is willing and life lasts long
enough,[48] there is hope of locating them and sending them
to you.

You see that I have replied in my own special prosaic style,
since we should strive to gain the thoughts rather than to gape
with astonishment at words, in order that our speech may
retain the simplicity of the Gospels and flee the froth of pagan
eloquence. Now, the extreme length of the letter compels
me to be silent.[49] I had hoped that I might embrace you
hand to hand that we might learn or teach some things by
talking together; at least, this is not impossible for Almighty
God, in whom no word is difficult.[50] Yet, daily, I hope for an
end to the illness of my mortality.

I should prefer that, if God grants what I have said above,
our occupation should turn on the allegorical interpretation
of questions and their mystical understanding and on the use
of the Old Testament for the affirmation of the New, rather
than that our investigation should consist in superficial historical interpretation, so that truly "deep calls unto deep in
the roar of your cataracts,"[51] because the one takes precedence
in time, the other in dignity. This is the food of the Christian
soul: the soul feeds on those things in which it delights; I hold
your ability in admiration and gaze with awe on the infinite
equipment of your vocabulary.[52]

Well done! When the beginnings you produce are so great,
what will be the fruit produced by Fructuosus?[53] In addition
to this good, since you also possess zeal for the divine Scriptures, especially in mutual discussion, you will soon send out

48 Cf. 2 Kings 4.16.
49 Jerome, *Letter* 7.6 (CSEL 54.31).
50 Cf. Luke 1.37.
51 Ps. 41.8 quoted in Jerome, *Letter* 120 praef. (CSEL 55.473).
52 Jerome, *Letter* 58.11 (CSEL 54.540).
53 Jerome, *Letter* 60.13 (CSEL 54.538); a triple play on the name of his
    correspondent: "qualia existent Fructuosi fructuosa frumenta"? The
    thoughts in this paragraph are borrowed and adapted from Jerome,
    Letter 108 (CSEL 54.540) concerning St. Paula. Jerome also says here:
    "A tree is known by its fruits."

branches and will bear grapes of exceeding sweetness, to confer
fruits upon your own nature, and to furnish others with the
delight of their enjoyment. I shall not be content with anything mediocre from you. Believe love which speaks the truth,
saying: if at all possible, I wish you to be excellent and perfect in that which is given to others in part and revealed in
knowledge in part, for it is proper that at the end of the
world the chosen vessels[54] of Christ shall be prepared for the
struggle with Antichrist.

Please do not think that you are of little value because
you are, as you complain, "sunk low in the obscure lands of
the west," since the more you see that you are in obscurity,
the brighter you shine, in the words of the Lord to the
Pharisees: "If you were blind, you would not have sin."[55]
All no doubt realize that the closer we are to the light, the
more easily we see the imperfections of the body; and the
"true light, which enlightens every man who comes into the
world"[56] has shone upon the world at His death, and not
immediately at His birth. Hence, the prophet: "The people
who sat in darkness have seen a great light; upon those who
dwelt in the land of gloom, a light has shone."[57]

The province which is your home claims for itself an origin
in Greece,[58] which is the mistress of letters and learning; we
recall that it has been the birthplace of most eminent and
most learned men, among whom we may mention the priest
Orosius, the Bishop Turibius, Idatius, and Carterius, another
bishop of laudable old age and holy erudition.[59] Therefore,

---

54 Cf. Acts 9.15.
55 John 9.41.
56 John 1.9.
57 Isa. 9.1.
58 Cf. Isidore, *Etym*. 9.2.110-111 on *Gallaeci*.
59 All were alive in the first half of the fifth century; Orosius was
   mentioned earlier in this letter and is associated with Turibius of
   Astorga as an anti-Priscillianist; Idatius of Lemica in Portugal continued Jerome's *Chronicle;* Carterius is probably the one mentioned
   in Jerome, *Letter* 69.2 (CSEL 54.680).

you should boast of the overflowing grace of Christ rather than find fault with the slight productivity of that country.

Now, you see, since "love knows no rank,"[60] I have put more words than utility into my letter and, as someone has said: "While I strive to make a pitcher, my hands have produced a jar."[61] It remains only to ask that you and your fellow pilgrims and your poor in spirit deign to pray for me, a greater sinner than all other men, in case the inexhaustible piety of the Redeemer of men may be willing to absorb the floods of impurities of my crimes and misdeeds.

Farewell in the Lord, brother to me in love, my well-serving lord, my son in years, my colleague in dignity, and close to me in family ties.[62] Do you and yours pray for me; when you get an opportunity, be sure to send me a letter.

---

60 Jerome, *Letter* 7.6 (CSEL 54.31).
61 Cf. n. 16 on *Letter* 11.
62 Do these words mean either that Fructuosus was already a bishop or that he and Braulio were somehow related? A literal interpretation is less likely, if one observes that Madoz quotes similar words, "my dearest friend, my son in years, my parent in dignity," applied by Jerome, *Letter* 105.5 (CSEL 55.246) to Augustine.

LIFE OF ST. EMILIAN

(*Vita s. Aemiliani*)

Braulio, unworthy bishop, sends greetings to the priest Fronimian, man of God, my lord and brother.

(1) In the time of Bishop John, my lord of pious recollection and our common elder brother and teacher of holy living and doctrine, I had intended, in obedience both to his suggestions and to your requests, to put down with my pen, insofar as my own lack of knowledge and poor state of health permitted, a clear account of the life of the blessed priest Emilian, our unique father and patron and singularly chosen in Christ in our times, relying upon the credibility of the information which I knew had been collected in the testimony of the venerable abbot Citonatus, the priests Sofronius and Gerontius, and that holy woman Potamia, of blessed memory. But because my notes on his virtues were interrupted almost as soon as I began them by inattention, due to a large amount of administrative work, I soon became busy with various ensuing misfortunes and with the troubles of uncertain times, until I lost even the desire to write and could not give my attention to it although you yourself strongly urged it.

Now by divine will, it seems to me, wanting to examine a codex for something that occurred to my mind, I had it searched and, when a pile of books was being turned over, that long-lost report was unexpectedly found, though it was not being sought, since the zeal of the searchers had been completely dimmed by the scant hope of ever finding it. Since, as the prophet says: "I was found by those who did not seek me";[1] "my heart is glad and my soul rejoices,"[2] not with

---

1 Rom. 10.20.

113

eagerness to light the lamp, but with joy at finding the
drachma;[3] once again, not without dispensation from above,
as I believe, I have summoned my courage to win the reward
of my obedience and to comply with your very frequent
requests.

(2) Therefore, I have composed as best I could and in the
plain and clear style that is becoming to such things, a short
book on the life of this saint; I have made it brief that it may
be read as rapidly as possible in the celebration of his mass,[4]
and I have directed it to you, my lord, and have taken care
to place this letter of mine at the head of it as I submit it for
your approval, that you may inspect each detail and either
correct or disapprove anything which is displeasing to you.
If it is pleasing to you, you may keep it and circulate it to
anyone else whom you wish and may give thanks on my
behalf to our Creator, to whom belong all good things. My
task was to obey; yours will be to publish if you deem it
worthy. I have one request; if you think anything therein
should be corrected, let it be emended before it is published,
but do not start to find fault with it until you have first
found something which pleases you. Further, since that most
holy man, Citonatus the priest, and Gerontius are still alive,
I want everything that I have written therein to be brought
to their attention first and to be thoroughly discussed by
them and to be confirmed for my accuracy in mentioning
names and events. I have also added at the end of the book,
just as I received them from you last year, the miracles which
I learned had been performed in that same place. At your
request I have also transmitted a hymn for the feast of this
saint, composed in the iambic senarius meter;[5] I have con-

---

2 Ps. 15.9.
3 Cf. Luke 15.8.
4 In the Mozarabic ritual, lauds were read after the Gospel, followed by
   a sermon which sometimes explained the daily feast.
5 This hymn of 80 verses has been edited in C. Blume–G. M. Dreves,
   Analecta hymnica medii aevi 27.125. Its manuscript tradition is entirely
   separate from that of the *Life of Emilian.* Cf. Lynch, *op. cit.* 236-40.

sidered it superfluous to write a sermon for the same day, since it seems to me there can be no greater exhortation than an account of his virtues, and, if a sermon were added, it would take up so much extra time that it would weary the spirits of the hearers.

(3) Therefore, I beg of you, that what I have done may be found acceptable both to yourself, whose orders I have obeyed, and to him who has, by the veneration of his virtues, caused the aforementioned men to be moved to testify to what they have seen and has caused all of you daily to witness similar things. You have obtained your request that these matters be set down by me, and I for my part am eager to receive the reward for fulfilling your desire.

In order that this same feast may be celebrated with a common mass, I have given instruction for its composition to my beloved son, deacon Eugene,[6] not thinking it strange to me if he uses his own tongue (for he and I are closely bound in all our plans and thoughts) to perform my duty in paying honor to this most blessed man; also thinking that I should enjoy a common reward with him in this matter as I make him a common participant in other things. May the grace of Christ deign to keep your beatitude in good health and mindful of me.

[Here begins the book on the life and miracles of the saintly and most blessed Emilian, priest and confessor of Christ, written by the blessed Braulio, bishop of the see of Saragossa.]

CONTENTS

---

6 An *Office for St. Emilian's Day* was published in M. Férotin. *Le Liber mozarabicus sacramentorum* (Monumenta ecclesiae liturgica 6; Paris 1912) 603-08. Lynch, *op. cit.* 223-24, gives reasons for taking this as the work of Eugene.

(4) The marvelous deeds and miracles performed almost in our own day by the apostolic and most upright man, Emilian the priest, are so new that they urge us to relate them; yet, at the same time, so vast in scope that to recount them is frightening. How can the pen of a man who is bound to earthly things worthily reproduce the acts of a heavenly man, who, when compared to past ages, shines like the brightest star; who, when compared to the present, stands above all in his inimitable virtue? In my opinion, not even if the Tullian springs should flow and come bounding forth in copious veins of eloquence, and multiplicity of thoughts should furnish an abundant supply of words, could all those works of grace be revealed which Christ, "who alone does wondrous deeds,"[1] has performed and still is performing through him, from the time he began to despise the world until he departed from his body and from the world. When I perceive this, I am seized with fear, for my knowledge is scarce rather than copious, my words are sterile instead of fertile, and I am not unskilled in my lack of skill. Still, the truth of the promise of Christ drives out fear, for thus He promised and thus He instructed us: "Open wide your mouth, and I will fill it."[2] And again: "The Lord will give many powers to those who are the good messengers of the word."[3] These words, too: "For it is not you

1 Ps. 71.18.
2 Ps. 80.11.
3 Cf. Ps. 67.12.

who are speaking, but the Spirit of your Father who speaks through you,"[4] are especially appropriate to this case. Thus the mind arises and lays aside the weapons of fear, and lo, what it feared it strives to enter upon with firm step, boasting of Thy great might, O Christ, who allowed a beast of burden to speak with human words[5] and can also permit a man to use suitable expressions. Another important point, which especially seems to concern the citadel of my mind and the anchor of my hope, is that only by the receipt of this work and the rewards of its labors and in no other way can I find a kind of soap with which to cleanse my most soiled and polluted life,[6] exactly as it was very elegantly expressed by one of the old poets: "This work, this may possibly save me from the fire."[7]

(5) Last of all, it remains to state that I preferred to report these matters even in an inferior work rather than to hide them under a cloak of lingering silence, lest later generations lose confidence in the truth of matters which their predecessors long passed over without mention. But to reply briefly to those who try to display their eloquence, let them know that the scurrilous words of detractors are of little weight, since it is not vain verbosity that is set up as an example under ecclesiastical law for humble and lowly Christians, nor the frailness of human vexations, nor even the inflated pride of ostentation, but the sober, moderate, and weighty gravity of truth. It is much better to tell the truth without embellishment than to make eloquent tales out of lies. This is easily understood in the gospels of the Savior, which were preached to the people in simple language. Shall I, then, unskilled as I am, make fun of the eloquence of wise men? Not at all. What I disapprove of is the insubstantial levity of carpers, for I do not think honest, wise,

---

4 Matt. 10.20.
5 Cf. Num. 22.28.
6 Cf. Jer. 2.22.
7 Juvencus, *Libri Evangeliorum,* pref. 1.22 (CSEL 24.2).

and mature men can be angry with me for my enthusiasm for this task, men who are not unaware that in the house of God each one should make such offering as he is able, even to the "hair of goats";[8] but if they, too, want to speak on this subject, as I have already said, not only will there be no lack of material, but they will not even be able to describe everything. Therefore, although I have, to an extent, pursued the study of secular disciplines, I have completely neglected to observe it here, lest I might make it more difficult for the less learned to understand and might confound the camp of Israel with the tongue of Jericho.[9]

(6) As I am about to begin the topic which I have decided to discuss, I want to warn the reader and the listener not to approach eager for words, but to lend himself full of devotion; or if it is the former which he is seeking, let him straightway depart, lest he spend his time in idleness to no avail; but he who is anxious to know what follows should come devotedly to learn and should understand, first of all, that there are some things related here which ought to be followed completely by us or by anyone else, but there are some things conferred in such a singular fashion upon that most upright man that no one else may even approach them by way of imitation without great harm to himself;[10] these, however, through admiration of him should make us intent upon the praise of God; for each kind must seek the precepts of its own kind, but only they may gain the special gifts upon whom the Almighty orders them to be conferred. Even those skilled in the law hold this in the case of benefits received by decree of their rulers.

(7) I shall not go back very far, nor shall I praise his grandfathers and great-grandfathers, as rhetoricians would do, for, as they themselves would say, if he sprang from a humble

---

8 Num. 31.20.
9 Cf. Jos. 6.18.
10 Cf. chapter 23.

birth, he is all the more to be praised for having adorned the
lowliness of his race with a worthy character.

Chapter 1

So we may begin our account with his conversion to the
religious life and with Christ favoring and the blessed man's
own prayers aiding our efforts, we may start with his situation
about the twentieth year of his life. The venerable priests of
the churches of Christ, Citonatus of holy and purest life, and
Sofronius and Gerontius, priests in whom the Church has
unlimited faith, have related to us in a trustworthy account
what they themselves have seen. To these well-proved witnesses is added the testimony of the very holy woman Potamia,
of blessed memory, whose noble origin was ennobled by the
even nobler course of her life. I have, therefore, chosen these
four as witnesses of the miracles performed in the flesh,
omitting the testimonies of peoples and provinces over almost
all of Spain concerning this matter, for we must of necessity
pass over those which became so common that they were of
almost daily occurrence, since they cannot be comprehended
completely, as has been said, and if anyone wants to know
them, he will more likely believe what has been seen.

(8) Now, as I started to say, the following is the account
of the aforementioned witnesses concerning his conversion and
religious life: the future shepherd of men was a shepherd of
sheep and he made the sheep go before him to the green
places in the mountains and, as was the custom of shepherds,
he carried a cithara with him, lest, while he was tending his
flock, his mind might become heavy and unoccupied and in-
attentive; and when he arrived at a certain spot appointed
by the will of heaven, the Deity overcame him with sleep; the
Maker of clean hearts with His usual zeal skillfully fulfilled
His function and changed the material of the cithara into
an instrument of learning and filled the mind of the shepherd

with the urge to contemplate the supernal. When he was aroused, he meditated on the celestial life and left that country and hastened to a desert region.

Chapter 2

(9) Rumor had brought him word that a certain hermit named Felix, a most holy man to whom he might properly offer himself as a disciple, was then living in Castle Bilibium.[1] He hastened thither and came to him and readily offered himself as a servant and was instructed by him how to guide his steps unfalteringly towards the kingdom above. By this deed, I believe he showed us that no one can correctly guide his steps to the blessed life without the instruction of his elders, for this man certainly did not, nor did Christ instruct Paul, nor did the divine power allow Samuel to do any such thing, but it did permit this man to go to the hermit and Paul to Ananias[2] and Samuel to Heli;[3] even though each of them had already been inspired by the divine power by signs and words.

Chapter 3

(10) After he had received the best instruction from him in the road to life and had been enriched abundantly with the wealth of divine teaching and the treasures of salvation, he returned to his own country, filled with the grace of religious wisdom; thus he arrived at a place not far from the village of Vergegio,[1] where his glorious body now lies, and he very soon saw that the crowd of people who came to him would be troublesome.

---

1 Outside the city of Haro in the province of Logroño.
2 Acts 9.10-19.
3 1 Kings 3.

---

1 Modern Berceo in La Rioja.

Chapter 4

(11) He sought the heights as his eager spirit traveled lightly up the steep path, so that he seemed, as he guided his steps through the vale of sorrow, to be climbing Jacob's ladder,[1] as it were, from virtue to virtue, in heart as well as in body. When he came to the more remote secret places of Mount Dircetius,[2] he stayed as close to its peak as the nature of the weather and the forest permitted, and became a guest of the hills, deprived himself of the consort of men and partook only of the consolations of the angels, and remained there for forty years. What invisible battles he experienced there, what visible ones, what temptations he endured of various ingenious kinds, what mockeries he experienced from the ancient scoundrel, only those can understand who themselves claim to have experienced them; there he directed all his emotions, there all his desires, there all his inspirations, there constantly all his course, in the way where he first directed his unyielding determination of holy devotion.

What a great gift! What a remarkable man! What an outstanding soul, so dedicated to contemplation of the divine that the present world can claim no room for itself therein! How often, I imagine, he must have been filled with divine ardor there among the thick and lofty forests and the tall peaks of the hills and the ridges reaching up to the sky, and must have said to Christ in a loud voice: "Woe is me that my dwelling is prolonged"![3] How often he would shout with sobs and sighs: "I desire to depart and to be with Christ"![4] How often he would be moved to the innermost parts and ardently lament, saying: "While I am in this body I am exiled from the Lord"![5] Meanwhile, he was shaken with cold,

---

1 Gen. 28.12, 13.
2 Now Sierra de la Demanda.
3 Cf. Ps. 119.5, 6.
4 Phil. 1.23.
5 Cf. 2 Cor. 5.6.

left destitute in solitude, drenched with incessant rain, troubled by the blasts of winds; yet he not only endured, but even delighted in, and longed for the bite of cold, the somber hours of solitude, the violent onrush of the rain, the severity of the winds, on account of the love of God, the contemplation of Christ, and the grace of the Holy Spirit. But since a city that is placed on a mountain cannot long remain hid,[6] the report of his holiness spread so far and wide that almost everyone learned of it.

Chapter 5

(12) When this was also reported to Didymus, who was then filling the office of bishop in Tarazona, he sought out the man and desired him to receive ecclesiastical orders, for he was in his diocese.

At first it seemed to him a difficult and serious thing to flee back and to return and to be led back almost from heaven to the world, from that quiet that had almost been attained to laborious duties, to be transferred from the contemplative to the active life; finally, he was forced against his will to obey in being appointed to the office of priest in the church at Vergegio. Then, he abandoned all the things to which men of that rank, at least in our times, are usually devoted, and he spent all his holy devotion upon this life to which he had been returned, persisting, however, in continuous prayers, week-long fasts, constant watches, genuine sagacity, definite hope, great frugality, kindly justice, firm endurance, and, to put it briefly, he abstained completely and unweariedly from every evil thing. He succeeded so well in gathering from the fields the flowers of the wisdom of ineffable divinity that he who had barely memorized the first eight Psalms now incomparably and most outstandingly surpassed the ancient

---

6 Cf. Matt. 5.14.

philosophers of the world in skill, wisdom, and ability, and
deservedly so, for what they achieved by worldly industry,
he was granted by the divine graces from above, so that it
seems fair for me to conjecture that, in his calling and education and miraculous deeds, he was in all respects similar to
Saints Antony and Martin. But to pass over much, among
his other ecclesiastical pursuits his greatest endeavor was
strenuously and zealously to drive wicked Mammon from the
temple of the Lord as fast as possible. Wherefore he spent
the substance of Christ upon the heart of Christ,[1] making
the Church of Christ rich in virtues rather than in wealth,
in religion rather than in income, in Christians rather than
in property. He knew that Christ would consider him guilty,
not for loss of temporal things, but for loss of men's souls.

Chapter 6

(13) For this reason, as is the custom of wicked clerics,
some of his clerics went to the bishop for the purpose of bringing accusations against him for the loss of their property, and
they found fault because the church was suffering ruin and
the property it had received was being completely squan-
dered. The aforementioned bishop was enflamed with the
torch of anger and possessed with envy because of the man's
virtues. Looking at the man of God, he vehemently attacked
him, and after he had belched forth the excess of his anger,
as a mind drunk with rage will do, the noble man of God
stood unmoved and as calm as ever, fortified with holiness
and protected by endurance. Thereupon he was relieved of
the ministry which he had assumed some time before and
spent the rest of his life undisturbed in the place which is
now called his oratory. So much for his conversion and re-

---

1 The old Spanish versions interpret this as giving the wealth of the
Church to the poor, who are the "heart" of Christ.

ligious life; and although those graces which were concealed (the new struggles which the Lord instituted and for which we have been instructed in faith and truth by Paul, the teacher of the Gentiles) were more wonderful than those which were brought to light by the gifts of the various virtues, even the latter were far too numerous to be fully described; yet I must, however unworthy my pen, describe the miraculous signs whereby his glory shone forth.

Chapter 7

(14) It happened one day that the enemy of the human race met the wrestler of the Eternal King on a journey and challenged him with these words: "If you would like to see what each of us can accomplish with his strength, let us have a contest." Barely had he finished speaking when he approached the saint and touched him in visible and corporeal reality, and for some time tried his wavering opponent, but the latter pressed Christ with prayers, and the divine aid strengthened his trembling steps and straightway caused the fugitive, apostate spirit to vanish into air. If it seems incredible to anyone that an invisible spirit can become substantial, save in the mystical sense, let it be explained to him how the divine pages narrate the struggle of Jacob with the angel, and a good angel, too.[1] I have this to say: that it would require less boldness for Satan to tempt a servant than the Lord, Emilian than Christ, man than God, the creature than the Creator.

Chapter 8

(15) But to return to my story, a certain monk named Armentarius was afflicted with pain and swelling of the stom-

---

1 Cf. Gen. 32.24; Osee 12.4.

ach and devotedly went to him to be cured. As soon as he put his hand upon the tumor and made the sign of the cross, straightway the illness left him and he blessed the Lord for the recovery of his health.

Chapter 9

(16) A certain woman named Barbara was brought from the territory of Amaia, contracted and in severe pain from a paralytic disease, and by the prayer of this saint was restored to her former health.

Chapter 10

(17) Then another woman was brought from the same territory, carried on a wagon because she was lame and had long lacked the use of her feet, and demanded to be cured by him. Now, it was Lent, and he was unwilling to see her because of his reverence for the season, for it was his custom to spend these days alone in his cell and he never saw anyone except one man who brought him a very small quantity of cheap food to sustain his life. Although he refused to see her, as I have said, she eagerly insisted that he at least be kind enough to allow her to kiss his staff; when the man of God heard this, he immediately directed that this should be done; as soon as she saw it, she prostrated herself before it and kissed it, and stood up firmly on her cured and strengthened feet, gave thanks for the divine gift, and straightway departed in joy.

Chapter 11

(18) The maidservant of senator Sicorius had for a long time been deprived of her sight and asked that the use of her eyes might be restored to her by him. Then the man of God

spoke and touched her under Christ's inspiration and ordered her to be cured. Straightway she followed his commands, recovered her sight, and beheld the shapes of objects in very clear light.

Chapter 12

(19) One who had been thrown out of his office as deacon had a violent seizure from an obstinate demon and was forced by others to stand before the blessed man's face to be cleansed. As he was being driven to hydrophobic frenzy by his madness and was foaming at the mouth, the unclean spirit was ordered by the holy man to depart from him. Straightway the disobedient learned to obey, was afflicted with invisible punishment, and made itself a stranger to the domicile which it had seized, while the man thus set free spoke forth loud praises to God.

Chapter 13

(20) Sibila, servant of a certain Tuentius, had been seized by impure spirits. He was dragged by his family to the blessed man who immediately asked by how many he was possessed. The spirits indicated that they were five, and each of them gave his own name, whereupon he gave them orders by the power of Jesus Christ, and they all departed straightway in great fright and very noisily, and he, cured, made a happy return to his family.

Chapter 14

(21) There was also a servant of Count Eugene, who had been tainted and afflicted by a spirit which had long possessed and enslaved him; yet, by the incomparable power of the divine omnipotence, he rendered him whole.

Chapter 15

(22) Now, what shall I say of the senator Nepotianus, and his wife Proseria, except that, as they were bound together in marriage, so also were they bound by a demon, so that the body which had become one in the ties of marriage was believed to be inhabited by a single spirit? The perverse one seemed to be in full control by virtue of having established this double possession. How well their state of health had been made known may be judged from the fact that it was so well publicized that it was not forgotten for several generations; lest it seem unnecessary, I may say that I have inserted it here, because everyone of the Cantabrians must either have seen it or heard about it. When the word came to our Emilian, he ordered the unclean enemy to leave the bodies of the aforementioned persons; not being able to disobey his order, it freed them as commanded, and both of them sang praises to the King of the heavens for their freedom.

Chapter 16

(23) Likewise, a demon had seized in most terrible fashion the daughter of the curial, Maximus, named Columba, and she had an unforeseen instability of her limbs and came to the presence of the servant of God with great hope of being cured. After he traced the sign of the cross on her forehead, the demon was straightway driven out and cast forth and she was cured of her poor health.

Chapter 17

(24) A most evil and quarrelsome demon was oppressing the house of the senator Honorius, usurping the rights of the master of the house in such monstrous fashion that every day

it committed some most disgraceful and most disgusting acts and no one could endure the fiend; it often happened that when the master and his household had taken their places for dinner, the unclean spirit brought in on platters the bones of dead animals and even their ordure; frequently, at night, when all were resting, it would steal the clothes of the men and women and hang them from the roofs, as if to conceal some shameful deed. Honorius became quite worried and did not know what to do, but amid his spiritual trials, he received an uplifting thought and became confident in the virtues of the man of God, and his hopes were so aroused that he sent to summon him and provided vehicles for his transportation. The messengers arrived and begged him to come and drive out the demon by whatever means he could. Finally he was persuaded by their entreaties to display the power of our God and set out on foot, not in a vehicle. When he reached Parpalines (where the events were taking place), he found everything just as it had been described to him; in fact, he experienced a few troubles there himself. He declared a fast, collected all the priests who lived in that region, and on the third day, when the vow of the ordained fast had been completed, he exorcized some salt and mixed it with water after the manner of the church and began to sprinkle the house; then the jealous demon burst forth from the interior of the house and finding itself cast forth and driven out of its abode, it threw stones at him, but he was fortified with an invincible shield and so remained unharmed. Finally the spirit fled, belching flames with a very sickening odor, and reached the desert, and so the inhabitants of that house rejoiced that they had been freed by the holy man's prayer.

Chapter 18

(25) In short, this man was so full of holiness, gave so much attention to the divine virtue, and possessed such command

of authority from above that when he was met by a throng of ·
people possessed of demons, he not only did not show the
slightest trace of fear, but he even shut himself up alone with
all of them, when he was about to cure them with the aid
of divine grace. Often, when he lay down on his bed, the
demons tried to set fire to him and they brought lighted
straw up to his bed, but it lost all its fire when they tried
to apply it; this they attempted all night long, laboring in
vain, and when he realized it, he forced these mad creatures
to tie each other with chains, and their own hands provided
the means of safety, at the same time that their hearts were
filled with madness.

Chapter 19

(26) I must not keep back a story which I perceive now is
well known to everyone: I am speaking of that beam which
was carefully fashioned and manufactured and taken to be
used for the construction of a granary, but which, when
measured with the other beams prepared for the same job,
was found to be too short. When he learned of this, he told
the workmen to go and have their dinner and not to worry,
while he withdrew to send his prayers before the eye of the
Creator. When he had finished his office at the sixth hour in
his own special but usual way, he knew that his wish had been
granted; he returned to the contractors and said: "Do not
think that you have been cheated of the success of your task.
Put the beam in its place." They lifted it and placed it as
he said and discovered that it was longer than the rest; that
it had increased more than a palm's breadth, whereupon they
made a mark that is still clearly visible today; and so through
his prayer, the contractors neither performed their labor without success nor were cheated of the reward of their task. The
beam itself is still today a source of cures for the faithful sick
and is reputed to possess so many virtues that hardly a day goes

by without its providing a cure for those who are ill, concerning which my story would become extremely long if I wanted
to reveal all the miraculous healings that are known to have
been performed there. Now I think it is worthwhile to touch
briefly upon his generosity and his chastity.

Chapter 20

(27) On one occasion, when crowds of needy came to him
demanding their usual small donation, although he did not
have or could not obtain anything to distribute, he did not
fail his inborn piety, but cut off the sleeves of his tunic and
generously offered them along with the cloak which he was
wearing. Then, one who was bolder than the rest, as beggars
will be, went up in front of the others and took what was
offered and put it on. Lo, here is a second Martin, who in
giving his cloak to the poor man clothed Christ! It is most
fitting that they who had a common spirit of liberality should
have achieved a common reward. But that the importunity
demonstrated in the presence of such a great man might not
pass without punishment, the rest of the beggar's companions
saw what he had done and became jealous. Indignant at the
presumption of one man, they armed themselves with sticks
and rose up and attacked him all together, and they drove
him here and there as each one's anger directed; he clearly
deserved this beating for his lack of precaution.

Chapter 21

(28) I will tell you of another incident which I should like
to use as a means of instructing the greedy that they should
have no thought for the morrow: it happened that a crowd of
people gathered at a time when the blessed man had very
little wine, but, since those who ask of the Lord shall not

lack every good thing,[1] a huge multitude was more than satisfied, they say, out of only a pint. A still greater story is told
of what happened on another occasion.

Chapter 22

(29) As his reputation for sanctity spread, large crowds of
visitors would come every day to see the man of God, whereupon he, of his own will, invited them to stay awhile as his
guests, that he might show his charity, and to refresh themselves. When his servant realized this, he told him that there
was nothing left for them to eat. He gently reprimanded the
servant and reproved his want of faith,[1] then prayed to Christ
to provide the necessary food. Before he had finished his
devotion, in through the gate came wagons copiously loaded,
sent by senator Honorius. The beloved of God received the
gift and gave thanks to the Creator of the world for this
answer to his prayers. He set out enough food for all who
were invited and ordered the rest to be laid aside for those
who came unexpectedly. He succeeded so well in striking
a mean course between the demands of hospitality and his
own continence that while at no time of day did his table
lack food for the guests, yet he was so strict and parsimonious
that he was never seen when not sober of mind and emaciated
of body. Those who came to him he refreshed in body with
food and in spirit with words. He was so clever in arguing
from comparison and so subtle in persuading the virtues of
the spiritual life that anyone who approached him for any
reason whatever went away improved and satisfied, while he
himself never departed in word or deed from his teaching and,
to make it brief, won such a great victory in overcoming the

---

1 Cf. Matt. 7.7.

---

1 Cf. Matt. 8.6., *et al.*

flesh that his north was never conquered and used to light a boiling caldron[2] nor was he offered as food to the fires of Nabuchodonosor.[3]

Chapter 23

(30) Now, these apostate spirits decided to use possessed beings to trouble him with slander, so clever are they in their wickedness. There were indeed no objections they could make against this servant of Christ, but they tried to reproach him with cohabiting with virgins of Christ. Thus, the ancient enemy uses his long-acquired skill to delude, for rumor can taint where there are no deeds to cause a man's downfall; if he cannot sway one's conscience, he can defame one's life, using his seductive charms to provide examples of consolation to those who think that no one is good and who despair of finding anyone to imitate in good deeds; so they think it some solace for their own punishment if no one can be found who is innocent, and they console their own damnation by the multitude of those who also perish.

Of what advantage can it possibly be to you, schemer of evils, to give an ill name to the servants of Christ, when the Lord has already promised them the kingdom of heaven, "in honor and dishonor, in evil report and good report"?[1] As a matter of fact, that holy man was devoted to abstinence and humanity even in his old age. He lived with holy virgins and, from his eighteenth year on, suffering from his holy labors and from physical pain, he calmly accepted, as a father might, all the services of the maidservants of God; yet, at the same time, as I have already said, he was so remote from base emo-

---

2 Cf. Jer. 1.13, 14. The sense is not clear, but presumably the author means that, though exposed to danger, as Jeremiah was from the north, Emilian never succumbed.

3 Cf. Jer. 21.7, 14.

---

1 2 Cor. 6.8.

tions that he never experienced a trace of dishonorable passion during those years. As he became still older, his physical needs became so great, since he was suffering from dropsy, that he could allow these same holy women to wash his body; yet, he never felt any forbidden desire. This, surely, is the special grace that has been conferred on very few, one which should not be attempted by anyone else, lest his rashness lead to danger. "Let every man remain before God in the calling in which he was called."[2] For David said: "Neither have I walked in great matters, nor in things too sublime for me."[3] He does walk in wonderful things above himself who attempts to perform what has not been granted him by divine power.

Chapter 24

(31) I shall also report how robbers fear him and thieves are made wary by him. A certain Simpronianus and Turibius were instigated and provoked by the devil to go and rob the house of the man of God, and, although it is written of the just man: "No evil shall befall you, nor shall affliction come near your tent,"[1] still they, for his chastisement or edification, were allowed to approach him, but were not allowed to chastise him—indeed they saw the plague turned by divine will against themselves. When these thieves got to the house of the holy man, they found outside the animal which he used to ride to church and secretly drove it away; but they did not long enjoy their thievery, for, after a little while, they returned, each one having lost an eye, begging for pardon and leading the animal back. But the holy one of God took the horse, blamed himself for owning it and straightway

2 Cf. 1 Cor. 7.20.
3 Cf. Ps. 130.1.

1 Ps. 90.10.

sold it and delivered its price to the poor, but he did not restore their eyes to the thieves, being warned, I suppose, by his good judgment, lest they might not cease from such wicked deeds if they were not deprived of their eyes, and that if they ever tried to do anything similar, they would be betrayed out of their hiding places by their physical marks and the reputation of their names; for who would think that he could not have had this granted him by the Lord, if one recalls that he often restored sight to the blind, both while living and after his death? Further, it was better that they should be punished for their deed in life than after life on this principle: "It is better to enter into the kingdom of heaven with one eye, than, having two eyes, to be cast into hell fire."[2]

Chapter 25

(32) About a year before his death, in the one hundredth year of his life, when it was revealed to him that he was about to end his human labors and to realize the most holy promises of the Almighty, he turned to an even more austere way of life; though he had already purified his limbs with fasts and watches, he entered this new campaign like a veteran soldier, so that his end might be more excellent, of the kind that is always more praiseworthy and more grand in the judgment of Christ, who said: "Whoever perseveres to the end, he shall be saved."[1]

Chapter 26

(33) In that same year during Lent the downfall of Cantabria was also revealed to him, for which reason he sent a

2 Cf. Matt. 18.9; Mark 9.46.

1 Matt. 24.13; cf. Matt. 10.22.

messenger to the senate to meet on the holy day of Easter.
They assembled at the time appointed. He related to them
what he had seen: he accused them of their sins—murders,
thefts, incests, acts of violence, and other crimes; he preached
that they should do penance for all of these; although all rever-
ently paid attention to him (for he was venerable to them
all as one of the disciples of our Lord Jesus Christ), one
senator named Abundantius said he must be delirious from
old age. Whereupon the holy man denounced him, predicting
that he would himself experience what was actually brought
to pass, for he was killed by the avenging sword of Leovigild.
As for the rest, since they did not repent of their wicked ways,
he used the impending divine anger in the same way to attack their perjury and deceit, and he was spattered with
their blood.

Chapter 27

(34) As the hour of his death clearly approached, he summoned a most holy priest, Asellus, with whom he was associated and in whose presence that most blessed soul was released from the body and returned to heaven.[1] Then, this
same holy man had the body carried with a large attendance
of religious and laid, where it still remains, in his oratory.

Farewell, farewell, blessed Emilian; now free from mortal
labors and enjoying your reward with the pious, be mindful
of unworthy Braulio who has related your story; aid me as
intercessor, that I may through you find pardon, for I am
unable to escape my evils; may I deserve this reward in exchange: that my prayers for the indulgence of my sins may
be heard through the favor of him whose virtues my pen
has described, and that I may be found worthy in the last
judgment, along with these over whom I unworthily preside
with pastoral care.

---

1 Nov. 12, 574.

I realize that the end of my book is getting close, but after telling of the wonderful things which he performed in his life, why should we be silent about the gracious gifts which he possesses after death? I shall publish two or three miracles to make more credible the testimony which has been narrated and sworn in writing by others.

Chapter 28

(35) How many blind were restored to sight at the tomb of this saint from the time of his death down to our own day, how many possessed of demons were purged, or how many suffering from various illnesses were cured—to tell this would require far too much space to be included in this book; I think it worth putting down that, immediately after his death, two blind people recovered their sight.

Chapter 29

(36) Only last year, as the feast of St. Julian the Martyr[1] was approaching and there was no "oil to make lights,"[2] they did not light the taper; yet, when they rose for vigils, they found the lamp full of oil and burning, so that it not only served them for light until morning, but was so abundant that it continued to multiply more and more miracles.

Chapter 30

(37) A woman named Eufrasia was brought there from a place called Banonicus, lame and blind, but her faith was

---

1 Perhaps Julian of Antioch, March 16.
2 Exod. 5.6.

whole, and as may be gathered from the following, even outstanding and illustrious: she anointed her eyes and her feet
and immediately the propitious divinity granted her to see and
to walk. Those who see these things performed in our own
times may believe what has been reported by witnesses;
even the place where she lives and the woman herself, recently
infirm but now whole, are known.

Chapter 31

(38) There was another girl about four years of age who
was brought from the Prato district, not far from his oratory,
seized with such a severe malady that she was close to death:
her parents, being pious and in fear of losing their child,
decided that she should be carried to the tomb of the blessed
man of God; so they took her, but she appeared to have died
on the way. But their faith did not fail them and they carried
her lifeless body and laid it at the altar, and, as evening came
on, they departed and left no one with her. After the space
of three hours, partly from curiosity, partly from sorrow,
they returned to see what the Creator had decided to do with
her: the girl they had left dead they found alive, and not only
alive, but playing with the altar cloth. They magnified Christ,
founder of all things, who had compassion on their devotion
and affliction.

Lo, here is a second Eliseus in recent times and in our own
age, whose dead bones give life to lifeless limbs,[1] the difference
being that, in his case, they timidly fled, while in this, they
were full of faith when they carried the dead girl in and laid
her at the altar. This, then, is the thought that is to be derived, that the one and the same God of the Old and the New
Testaments, our Lord Jesus Christ, "who alone does wondrous
deeds,"[2] in those days concealed "the hope of happiness from

---

1 Cf. 4 Kings 13.20, 21.
2 Ps. 71.18.

those who feared him,"[3] from those who trembled with fear under the law and from those not yet confirmed in love "which casts out fear, because fear brings punishment,"[4] but now the virtue which alone awakens the dead has made perfect by the grace of faith those who hope in Him with a good conscience; yet, not only the time, but the reasons for bringing their dead are different: the former brought them to bury them, the latter to recover the living. From this it is possible to understand how great is the blessed repose won there by holy men at whose tombs Almighty God performs so many wonderful things.

We have fulfilled our promise; it remains to bring to an end the course of our account and to offer thanks to Christ, the King of the heavens, by whose aid and inspiration we have seen this work undertaken and completed, who, for the sake of our present miseries, has granted us the contemplation of the lives of holy men, who lives with God the Father and the Holy Spirit, one through all ages. Amen.

---

3 Cf. Ps. 30.20.
4 1 John 4.18.

LIST OF THE BOOKS OF ISIDORE, COMPILED BY BRAULIO, BISHOP OF SARAGOSSA[1]

(*Renotatio Isidori a Braulione Caesaraugustano episcopo edita*)

Isidore, a man of eminence, bishop of the church at Seville, successor and brother of Bishop Leander, flourished from the time of the Emperor Mauritius and King Recared; in him antiquity gained some new fame for itself, or rather our age saw in him an image of antiquity, for he was a man well trained in every kind of locution, so that the quality of his words made him adaptable for one who was learned and for one who had no knowledge, famous both for suiting his words to his subject and for his incomparable eloquence. It can now be very easy for any prudent reader to judge how great his knowledge was from his varied interests and carefully written works. I have set down the following comments about those works which have come to my notice. He published:

(1) Two books of *Differences,* in which he made subtle distinctions between the meanings of words which are commonly confused in practice.

(2) One book of *Introductions,* in which he described, with brief notes, the contents of each book of Holy Scripture.

(3) One book *On the Lives and Deaths of the Fathers,* in which, by means of brief sentences, he set forth the deeds, greatness, death, and burial of each.

(4) Two books of *Offices* for his brother, Bishop Fulgentius, in which he revealed the origin of offices and why each one is

---

1 Cf. Introduction, p. 8.

performed in the Church of God, interpreting with his own pen, but not omitting the authority of the elders.

(5) Two books of *Synonyms,* in which reason appears to exhort the soul to consolation and to the hope of obtaining pardon.

(6) One book to King Sisebut *On the Nature of Things,* in which he settled some obscure points about the elements after investigating both ecclesiastical teachers and philosophers.

(7) One book *On Numbers,* in which he touched, in part, upon the science of arithmetic to explain the numbers inserted in ecclesiastical writings.

(8) One book *On the Names of the Law and the Gospels,* in which he explained the mystical significance of the persons mentioned.

(9) One book of *Heresies,* in which he followed the examples of our elders and collected scattered topics as briefly as possible.

(10) Three books of *Sentences,* adorned with choice selections from the books of Pope Gregory's *Morals.*

(11) One book of *Chronicles* from the beginning of the world to his own time, collected with extreme brevity.

(12) Two books *Against the Jews* at the request of his sister, Florentina, a nun of saintly life, in which he expressed, by quotation from the Law and the Prophets, approval of everything which the Catholic faith believes.

(13) One book of *Famous Men,* to which I have added the present remarks.[2]

(14) One book of *Monastic Rule,* which he most properly tempered for use in his own country and to suit the spirits of the weak.

(15) One book *On the Origin of the Goths,* and the *Kingdom of the Sueves,* and also the *History of the Vandals.*

(16) Two books of *Questions,* which furnish the reader with much material from ancient commentators.

2 This is the evidence that the *List* was intended as a supplementary chapter to Isidore's *De viris illustribus.*

(17) A manuscript of *Etymologies,* of extremely large size,
set off by him by subject matter rather than in books;
because he wrote it at my request, I divided it into fifteen[3]
books, although he left it unfinished. This work is suitable
to every branch of philosophy; whoever reads and meditates
upon it frequently will have and deserve a reputation for
knowledge of both divine and human affairs. It is packed
with elegant statements of many kinds, collected in concise
manner; from it, there is practically nothing that cannot be
learned.

There are many other smaller works of this man, as well
as some well-embellished inscriptions in the church of God,
for God created him in recent times to support His Church
after so many disasters in Spain. (I presume it was to restore
the monuments of the ancients, lest we grow dull from boorish
rusticity.) Not unfittingly may we apply to him the words
of the philosopher who said: "As we journeyed and wandered
like strangers in our own city your books have, as it were,
brought us home, so that we may occasionally know who and
where we are. You have revealed the history of our fatherland, the revelations of all time, the sacred laws, the laws
of the priests, public and private discipline, the names, kinds,
functions, and origins of sees, regions, places, and all things
divine and human."[4] With what a flood of eloquence, with
what barbs of Divine Scriptures and proofs from the Fathers
he confounded the heresy of the Acephalites, is revealed
in the acts of the Council which met under his leadership at
Seville, in which he established the Catholic[5] truth against
Gregory, the leader of the said heresy. He died in the time
of the Emperor Heraclius and the most Christian King Chintila, ranking above all others for his sane doctrine, and having performed more works of charity than anyone else.

3 Reading *quindecim* with Galindo instead of *viginti,* as in later texts.
4 Cicero, *Acad. post.* 1.3, as quoted in Augustine, *De civ. Dei* 6.2. Cf.
Introduction, p. 10.
5 *cam,* an abbreviation for *catholicam,* is Galindo's very probable correction of the manuscript reading *eam.*

WRITINGS OF
FRUCTUOSUS OF BRAGA

INTRODUCTION

HE MOST IMPORTANT SOURCE for our knowledge of the life of St. Fructuosus of Braga is the *Vita sancti Fructuosi*, written probably not long after his death by an unknown author. The present account is almost wholly dependent upon the edition and English translation of the *Vita* by Sister Clare Frances Nock.[1] The work gives us no means, direct or indirect, of finding a single date for the life of Fructuosus, for no attention is paid to exact chronology. Internal evidence is of no help at all, since the several persons named in the text are otherwise unknown and the references to the king and the temporal powers, while numerous, are vague. Fortunately, the few outside sources are specific.

A letter written to Braulio and the latter's reply have been translated above;[2] these can be placed early in the year 651, just before Braulio's death. Fructuosus was called by Braulio "collega dignitate," which, if taken literally, as Sister Clare Frances does, should mean that Fructuosus was a bishop, but it is to be noted that the words occur in a longer passage borrowed or paraphrased from Jerome; hence not too much emphasis should be placed on them. At some time between 653 and 656, Fructuosus became Bishop of Dumium, the suburb of Braga which had been founded by St. Martin. On December 1, 656, the Tenth Council of Toledo met, and one of its formal acts was to promote Fructuosus from Dumium to the metropolitan see of Braga: "Furthermore, by a unanimous vote of all present, we have elected the venerable Fruc-

---

1 *The Vita sancti Fructuosi* (Cath. Univ. of America, Studies in Mediaeval History, N.S. 7).
2 Pp. 96-112.

145

tuosus, bishop of the church at Dumium, to hold the reins
of the church at Braga, so that he may undertake the direction
of the whole metropolis of the province of Galicia, all the
bishops and peoples and assemblies therein, and the care of
governing all the souls oft he church of Braga."[3] A letter
from Fructuosus to King Receswinth falls into this same
period, so that all known dates of his activity are between
651 and 656. His birth may be placed very roughly close to
the year 600. The breviaries, which are generally reliable
and based on contemporary records, give the date of his death
as April 16, 665, but Professor Bishko believes that these breviaries have no historical warrant. Nothing is known for certain
of Fructuosus' work as archbishop.

If the *Vita* is vague in chronology, it is quite specific in
geographical references. It is agreed that the author knew
St. Fructuosus well, was possibly a disciple of his, and wrote
the biography not too long after the saint's death. The only
likely author whose name has been suggested is St. Valerius
of Bierzo and this is accepted in many Spanish and Portuguese
circles today, though far from universally. Sister Clare Frances, in a fully-documented chapter on the authorship of the
Vita, concluded that stylistic evidence alone is sufficient to
disprove this attribution.[4] The author of the *Vita s. Fructuosi*
must remain anonymous, but his account is of the greatest
value and interest.

The father of Fructuosus was an officer in the Spanish
army and possessed flocks in the valleys of the mountainous
regions where his son later started to found his monasteries.
After the death of his parents, the son became a cleric and was
trained by a certain Conantius, quite possibly the one known
to have been Bishop of Palencia from before 610 to after
636. His first independent act was to return to the country
where his father's flocks had been pastured and to found a

---

3 J. D. Mansi, *Sacrorum conciliorum nova et amplissima collectio*
11 (Florence 1765) 41.
4 *Op. cit.* 23-38.

monastery at Compludo, a little west of Astorga. He apparently named the monastery after Sts. Justus and Pastor, who were martyred in that place, for their feast day[5] was to be a special day in his community. Fructuosus used his extensive family inheritance for the founding and enrichment of this place and left, for the guidance of its monks, a very strict *Rule*, to be discussed later.

He then began a series of restless pilgrimages to other sites in the same general region, where he founded one monastic institution after another, traveling constantly to visit all of his foundations in northern and western Spain. The *Vita*[6] records that he finally became anxious to make a pilgrimage to the Orient, but that information of his intended departure was given to the king, who ordered him brought to Toledo, where he reluctantly gave up his plans, for the king feared "lest such a shining light should withdraw from Spain." It was apparently after this event that he settled in Dumium and Braga.

The most important of the surviving works ascribed to St. Fructuosus are two sets of monastic rules, the earlier one a specific *Rule* for the monks at Compludo (*Regula monachorum Complutensis*), and a later one a general or *Common Rule* (*Regula monastica communis*). To manuscripts of the latter is appended an unusual *Pact,* or form of monastic oath, which was at that time peculiar to Galicia. Finally, we have two letters written by Fructuosus, one found in the collection of Braulio's letters already translated,[7] and one to King Receswinth. None of these works of Fructuosus has previously been translated into English.

The Latin text followed here for the two *Rules* and the *Pact* is essentially that printed by Holste–Brockie,[8] as reprinted

---

5 August 6.
6 Ch. 17.
7 Pp. 96-99.
8 Lucas Holstenius, *Codex regularum monasticarum et canonicarum* 1 (Vienna 1759) 198-219.

in Migne, PL 87.1099-1132. This edition is far from satis-
factory, often corrupt, but no more recent study of the text
has been made from the manuscripts known to exist in Spain
and Portugal.[9] In addition to a few obvious emendations
of my own, all mentioned in the notes, it has been possible
to introduce a small number of corrections from two sources.
About the year 800 Benedict of Aniane studied all the
monastic *Rules* which had been compiled before his time
and arranged the various topics of each by subject matter in
a *Concordia Regularum*. His text of Fructuosus appears to
have been independent of that which is the basis of the Latin
in PL 87. This *Concordia* was edited by Ménard[10] and reprinted *in extenso* in PL 103.701-1380, with notes on a manuscript
of the French abbey of La Grasse, which contained the first
Rule of Fructuosus.[11] Further improvement of the text is
found in the Portuguese translations made by Caetano do
Amaral,[12] which have been very thoroughly examined by
Mário Martins, S.J.,[13] with an invaluable commentary.

It is not even certain what would be the exact titles of the
Rules as determined by the manuscript tradition, but the

9 The second *Rule* is found in a Munich manuscript, Lat. 28118, of the
ninth century. A photograph of the top half of f. 119, with parts of
chapters 2 and 3, may be seen in Z. García Villada, *Historia eclesi-
astica de España* II[1] (Madrid 1932) 308, accompanied by a Spanish
version of the first chapter. Important new material on existing
manuscripts of the *Rules* of Fructuosus is found in M. C. Díaz y Díaz,
"La tradición de la 'Regula Isidori,'" *Studia Monastica* 5 (1963) 27-57.
A statement of important problems that await solution will be found
in C. W. Barlow, "The Latin texts of the *Regulae* of Fructuosus of
Braga," *Bracara Augusta* 11-12 (1962) 43-46.
10 H. Ménard, *Concordia regularum auctore S. Benedicto Anianae abbate*
(Paris 1638).
11 An example of the independent value of Benedict of Aniane is shown
by his preservation of *saionibus,* referring to Visigothic public officials,
where the common text has more than once changed the unfamiliar
word to *senioribus.* The *Concordia* included the major portion of
both of the *Rules* of Fructuosus, but omitted about five chapters of
each and parts of other chapters which did not fit its systematic
classification.
12 *Vida e regras religiosas de S. Fructuoso Bracarense* (Lisbon 1805).
13 *O monacato de S. Frutuoso de Braga* (Coimbra 1950).

purpose of each is fairly clear from its contents. The first, *Regula monachorum Complutensis,* was written specifically as a guide for the monks in the first monastic foundation of Fructuosus at Compludo. The common text has 23 chapters, the last incomplete. In the chapter headings there are 25 titles in all and it is quite possible that some existing manuscripts still contain the original text of one or both of these chapters.[14]

The importance of the two *Rules* which come from Galicia was first studied by Professor C. J. Bishko in his Harvard doctoral dissertation, *Spanish Monasticism in the Visigothic Period* (1957). No similarly detailed treatment exists in any other place. The general works on monastic history neglect the important fact that in almost every respect Galician particularism departed from the peninsular norm. Compulsory enlistment of non-aristocrats as monks, secular possession of monasteries, and monastic synoecism all helped to turn the monasteries into a battleground. Fructuosan reforms had a strong constitutional basis.

The Compludo *Rule* possesses all the severity of its ascetic models in the examples of the Desert Fathers of Egypt and their sayings, introduced in Galicia by St. Martin of Braga.[15] It is definitely not Benedictine in character. Much of the material may be found in Pachomius, Cassian, Jerome, and especially Isidore, but the dependence is more in ideas than in direct borrowing of text.[16] The letter which St. Fructuosus wrote to Braulio shows a keen interest in locating the writings of his predecessors, Cassian in particular, and a romantic incident in the *Vita*[17] proves that in his travels Fructuosus generally had among his entourage one donkey loaded with

---

14 Cf. note at Ch. 23.

15 It is so severe that Pérez de Urbel, *Los monjes españoles de la edad media* I 430, remarks that it is difficult today to believe that there were men actually able to observe its regulations.

16 Details of this debt may be read in Pérez de Urbel, *op. cit.* 431-34, and in many notes of Caetano do Amaral, and in the several articles of Prof. Bishko, but no exact study of the sources of Fructuosus and his debt has ever been published.

17 Ch. 12.

bags full of manuscripts in the care of a special attendant. Quotations from both Old and New Testaments are frequent throughout and the aptness of the citations shows a thorough knowledge of the Scriptures. The words used are not infrequently different from those of the Vulgate; occasionally the quotation is worded so freely that it must have been made from memory.

There are indications that this first *Rule* was never thoroughly revised after it was composed or dictated. There is no attempt to put the topics in order by a logical sequence of chapters, and the titles of the chapters, possibly written many years later, do not always comprise every subject under each particular heading. The *Rule* prescribes many hours daily for reading, meditations, and prayer; it describes work in the fields and pastures and the assignment of tasks to those working in the kitchen or tending the sick or welcoming visitors; but there is not a word about a scriptorium, although the monks under Fructuosus certainly copied manuscripts for themselves and sought from other religious students texts which they did not have. (The library of Fructuosus, though this applies to his later years in a larger establishment, was big enough that it was possible for a book to be misplaced on its shelf or to be entirely lost.) Although this *Rule* does not cover every phase of life in a monastery, it is very vivid in the topics which it does handle and very revealing to a student of the cultural or economic life of the period.[18] It is dated by Bishko with considerable probability in the period between 630 and 635.[19]

The other *Rule* attributed to Fructuosus is called both in the title and in the text a *Common Rule*. In its earliest form it has been dated by Bishko as *ca.* 660. It seems possible that no manuscript will be found ascribing the work to Fructuosus,

---

18 Mário Martins, "A vida economica dos monjes de S. Frutuoso" and "A vida cultural de S. Frutuoso e seus monjes" (see Bibl. *infra*).
19 C. J. Bishko, "Spanish Monasticism in the Visigothic Period," Harvard University, *Summaries of Theses* (Cambridge 1938) 128.

but he could have had a part in this first redaction. If so, it envisages a much later period in the life of the bishop, after his numerous monasteries had been founded and others had sprung up beside them, and after a new branch of monasticism developed in which small rural proprietors often merged their holdings to form a sort of collective monastery. The *Common Rule* provides that the abbots and priors of monasteries in a particular neighborhood shall meet monthly, among other purposes to consider new legislation for those in their charge. Its 20 long chapters deal either with matters supplementary to the other *Rule* or with conditions which had arisen in later years, particularly with the large influx of whole families—men, women, and children—into monastery life. The *Common Rule* must have been published in more than one form with several additions. As it now stands, it certainly was intended to end after chapter 19, and the following chapter is a later regulation.[20] Once again, as in the *Rule* for the monks at Compludo, the contents deal so specifically and realistically with contemporary situations that the *Common Rule* is an important source for knowledge of relations between Church and state, between the secular and the religious life, in the western part of Spain in the middle of the seventh century.

The *Pact,* which is apparently appended to manuscripts of the *Common Rule,* is at once the most universal and most controversial of the writings attributed to Fructuosus of Braga. It was first studied in detail by Herwegen,[21] especially for its relation to numerous other monastic pacts. One cannot be certain that Fructuosus wrote any part of this *Pact,* or even that this particular one was in use in any of the monasteries under his control. The doctrinal beliefs required to be ac-

---

20 Bishko also shows that the first two chapters are a later addition. Again, the sources of this *Rule* have not been pursued with thoroughness. There must be other passages from earlier Rules and other examples of dependence on writers on monastic subjects, in addition to the passages obviously taken from Jerome.

21 *Kirchenrechtliche Abhandlungen* 40.

knowledged and the allegiance to the abbot demanded of those who profess the religious life are consistent with the regulations of Fructuosus, which require that adherents take some kind of an oath (and it is called several times a *pactum*) after one year of novitiate. The truly remarkable feature of this particular *Pact* is that, in cases of serious dispute, there may be a final appeal from the injustice of an abbot to other abbots, to the bishop, or even to the temporal ruler, if he is a Catholic. Strange to the certainly genuine regulations of Fructuosus, however, are provisions that a monk on trial for insubordination shall appear without cincture and without shoes, the controversial nature of the *Pact,* and the right of appeal in certain cases. The latter is a distinct feature of the laws derived from a Germanic code. The place of the *Pact* in contemporary Church history is stated by Bishko[22] in the following paragraph:

> The predominant Spanish, or, as we may call it, Visigothic monastic tradition was established throughout the peninsula before 711, except in Galicia, and it survived in the early Reconquista period. . . . It was a fairly typical pre-Benedictine Western cenobitism, accepting the normal monarchical abbatiate and episcopal supervision, but displaying a marked partiality for double houses and for the use not of a single Rule, but of *codices regularum* containing, *inter alias,* the Rules of Pachomius, Augustine, Basil, Isidore of Seville, Fructuosus of Braga, and, more rarely, Benedict. On the other hand, from the mid-seventh century on, in Galicia, there arose a powerful rival monastic tradition, the Gallegan, which undertook to limit episcopal control by monasticization of the episcopate ("episcopi sub regula") and which replaced the monarchical abbatiate by a quasi-feudal system of contractual relations between the abbot-*patronus* and monks-dependents. This peculiarly Gallegan concept was embodied in the *pactum,* the formal written covenant between abbot and monks, by which the latter, in choosing their abbot and legally submitting their persons to him along with a pledge of obedience, compelled the abbot to accept considerable limitation of his powers, including recognition of the legal right of rebellion on the part of his subjects. Since the bond was personal, *pacta* had to be renewed at each abbatial election, but new converts . . . simply subscribed to the current *pactum.*

22 *Speculum* 23 (1948) 579-80. Cf. also Bishko's study in *Estudios dedicados a Menéndez Pidal* 2.513-51, especially 515.

Herwegen and Bishko agree that the present example of a *Pact* is contemporary with the final publishment of the *Common Rule, ca.* 675.

The best edition of the *Letter* of Fructuosus to King Receswinth and his assembled bishops is found in an article by A. C. Vega,[23] from which the present translation is made. I have also checked for new information a note by W. Gundlach[24] and the same scholar's edition among the *Epistulae Wisigothicae*.[25] Vega also attempts to clarify the rather puzzling contents of this formal letter, which assumes knowledge of an incident that must have been clear when the letter was written. It is a plea for release of some political prisoners who have been held for a very long time, apparently since the days of King Chintila, who had reigned from 636 until his death in 638. Chintila established his position against many revolts and this is the probable period during which he imprisoned his political enemies; if so, they must have been confined for a full 25 years previous to this appeal of Fructuosus. The long second canon of the Second Council of Toledo, held late in 652, mentions refugees and the swearing of an inadvisable oath, providing a situation which had led Gundlach to date the letter of Fructuosus at this time. It seems best, accordingly, to conclude that the letter was written about 652, just previous to or during the Council meeting.[26]

Three poems, printed in PL 87.1129-1132, are almost certainly not directly from the hand of Fructuosus; hence they are not translated here.

---

23 *La Ciudad de Dios* 153 (1941) 335-45.
24 *Neues Archiv* 16 (1891) 45-46.
25 Monumenta Germaniae Historica, *Epp.* 3 (1892) 688-89.
26 A possible objection to 652 appears to me in the mention of the cruel reign of Chindaswinth, father of Receswinth; the father had first associated his son with himself and then virtually retired, but he did not die until 653. This would not, however, be the only case of a cleric openly mentioning with disfavor the acts of a living ruler.

BIBLIOGRAPHY

Barlow, Claude W. "The Latin texts of the *Regulae* of Fructuosus of Braga," *Bracara Augusta* 11-12 (1962) 43-46.

Bishko, C. J. *Spanish Monasticism in the Visigothic Period,* unpublished doctoral dissertation (Harvard 1937); *Summaries of Theses* (Cambridge 1938) 126-29.

——————. "Salvus of Alvelda and Frontier Monasticism in Tenth-Century Navarre," *Speculum* 23 (1948) 559-90.

——————. "Gallegan Pactual Monasticism in the Repopulation of Castile," *Estudios dedicados a Menéndez Pidal* 2 (Madrid 1951) 513-31.

do Amaral, C. *Vida e regras religiosas de S. Fructuoso Bracarense* (Lisbon 1805). The only copy known to be in America is at the Newberry Library in Chicago; I have a microfilm.

Gundlach, W. "Epistolae ad res Wisigothorum pertinentes," *Neues Archiv* 16 (1891) 9-48.

Gundlach, W., ed. "Epistolae Wisigothicae," Monumenta Germaniae Historica, *Epistolarum* 3 (Berlin 1892) 658-90.

Herwegen, I. *Das Pactum des hl. Fruktuosus von Braga* (Kirchenrechtliche Abhandlungen 40; Stuttgart 1907).

Martins, Mário. "A vida economica dos monjes de S. Frutuoso," *Brotéria* 44 (1947) 391-400.

——————. "A vida cultural de S. Frutuoso e seus monjes," *Brotéria* 45 (1947) 58-69.

——————. *O monacato de San Frutuoso de Braga* (Coimbra 1950); reprint from *Biblos* 26.

Migne, J. P. *Patrologiae latinae cursus completus* (Paris 1844-1864) 87, 103 (=PL).

Nock, Sr. Clare Frances. *The Vita sancti Fructuosi* (Catholic University of America, Studies in Mediaeval History, New Series 7; Washington 1946.)

Pérez de Urbel, J. *Los monjes españoles en la edad media* I (Madrid 1933) 377-450.

——————. "Vida y caminos del Pacto de San Fructuoso," *Revista Portuguesa de Historia* 7 (1957) 377-97.

Vega, A. C. "Una carta auténtica de San Fructuoso," *La Ciudad de Dios* 153 (1941) 335-45.

154

RULE FOR THE MONASTERY OF COMPLUDO

(Regula monachorum Complutensis)

CONTENTS

Chapter 1

After the love of God and of one's neighbor, which is the bond of all perfection and the greatest of the virtues, it has been determined by the tradition of the Rule that the following shall be preserved in monasteries: first, to be devoted to prayer night and day and to observe the prescribed division of hours; then, never for anyone to be idle in any respect or slothful in spiritual exercises in the daytime.

Chapter 2

The method of celebrating the first hour is sanctioned by the words of the prophet: "At dawn I shall stand by you and I shall see you. For you are a God delighting not in wickedness."[1] And again: "To you I shall pray, O Lord; at dawn you shall hear my voice."[2] The second hour too is set up as a sort of boundary between *Prime* and *Terce;* whence also it must not be spent in idleness by the monks. Hence it has been determined that it shall be celebrated with a threefold observance of Psalms, thus completing the office of *Prime* and subsequently climbing the steps towards *Terce.* Likewise it has been determined that this same order is to be observed in the case of the other hours, *Terce, Sext, None; Duodecima* also and *Vespers,*[3] so that, both before and after each of these three sets of regular hours, special prayers may continue the observances. During the night hours, the first hour of night is to be celebrated with six prayers and then

---

1 Cf. Ps. 5.4, 5.
2 Cf. Ps. 5.3, 4.
3 Reading *atque vespera;* the *Concordia* of Benedict of Aniane reads *usque vesperam,* "until evening," because *Duodecima* and *Vespers* may be identical. Du Cange quotes this example of *Duodecima* as equal to *Vespers,* but cf. ch. 6 below, p. 162, where a period of meditation is appointed "from *Duodecima* until *Vespers.*"

to be finished in the church by chanting ten Psalms with lauds and benedictions. Then, as they say farewell to each other and stand by one another in reconciliation and absolution, they shall make mutual forgiveness of their sins; and by humble piety those who have been separated from the company of the brothers because of slight faults shall earn forgiveness. Then finally as they go to their beds, all coming together as a sign of perfect peace and the absolution of sins, they shall sing three Psalms as usual with lauds and benedictions and shall recite together the Symbol of Christian Faith; that they may show the purity of their faith in the sight of the Lord, so that if by an unexpected though not unlikely circumstance, anyone should be called during the night hours to leave his body, he might offer before God a faith already tried and a conscience purified of every scandal. Then, going to their cells in deep silence and with composed countenance and quiet step, no one walking closer to another than the space of a cubit or even daring to look at another, each shall go to his bed. There, in silent prayer and meditation of Psalms, he shall complete his prayer with the recitation of Psalm 50 and a prayer; and without daring to make any noise or to whisper or even to clear his throat, he shall gratefully receive the quiet of the night's sleep.

Chapter 3

The prior shall stand in the center of the dormitory until all are quiet, and when all are reclining shall silently pass by the bed of each one, so that none may be slow in lying down or may idly engage in secret whispering against the Rule; and that, by observing the actions of each more closely, he may learn how to treat the character and merits of each. Likewise either a senior monk or one of the well-tried brothers shall assist him in the communal silence, until they have all become quiet, lest they air idle stories or devote themselves to jokes or become accustomed to any harmful pursuits. For it has been determined by the Rule that no monk shall talk in the dormitory, but if there are several together, they shall recite the Psalms, or if one is alone he shall meditate aloud. Likewise, arising before midnight, let them chant twelve Psalms in unison, according to custom. Before the rest arise, however, the prior shall be called by the brothers who are on watch, that the signal may be sounded with his blessing and that he may diligently visit the couch of each before they get up. This he is to do during all the night hours, so that the prior always arises before the others are told to get up, that he may see for himself how each one is sleeping, and that he may not incur any charges of immodesty through lack of supervision while he himself was asleep. After a brief period of rest, they shall observe the midnight office in which four responsories are recited after each group of three Psalms. Then, after midnight in winter, all shall sit down and one shall sit in the middle and read a book; and what is read shall be explained by the abbot or prior to those who understand less well. The same shall be observed in summer after *Vespers,* that a book be read before *Compline.* Then, having sung twelve more Psalms, they shall go to the dormitory and rest a little. When cockcrow sounds, after recitation of three Psalms with lauds and benedictions, they shall celebrate morning mass. When this is completed, since they are to devote themselves to meditation, as soon as they have come to the customary place of meditation, they shall recite three Psalms and a prayer and, when completely finished, they are to meditate until sunrise. At all prayers in each hour night and day at the end of all Psalms, they are to sing "Glory to God," and prostrate themselves on the ground, observing the custom that none shall bow down or arise before the elder, but all shall arise observing equality and shall pray with palms extended to heaven as all genuflect[1] together.

---

1 Reading *genuflectunt* for *merguntur.*

During the observance of Saturday and Sunday nights, adding a sixth office to the groups of Psalms, the watches shall be celebrated by six groups of Psalms with six responsories, that the solemnity of the Lord's Resurrection may be honored with more ample singing of Psalms in the office, which is always to be celebrated appropriately with special liturgy on the preceding night.

Chapter 4

Clothing shall not be abundant nor more than is necessary; each monk's absolute needs can be satisfied with two cowls, one shaggy, one smooth, and one mantle, and three undergarments, and two shirts. In the case of shoes, the custom to be followed is that those who wish may wear shoes in the winter from November 1 to May 1; but, in the summer months, they may be protected only with sandals. The wearing of trousers is allowed to anyone, especially to those who perform services at the altar. One who does not wish[1] to observe this custom is not to be reprehended, since there are many monasteries even in this area which have not yet adopted it.

A proper discipline is to be maintained as regards bedcovers[2] and no one is to require more than one coarse blanket, a thick wool covering, a mat, and two sheepskins. Anything that the monks possess in the manner of clothing is not to be kept by or belong to an individual, but is to be stored in one cell under the hand of a spiritual brother who, when anyone asks for a necessary article, shall provide on loan one of the proper size; and let no monk claim it as his own, saying: "My book, my notebook," etc. If any such words come from his mouth, he shall be subject to penance, that nothing in the monastery may seem like private goods, but rather that

1 Reading *noluerit* with *Concordia* for *voluerit*.
2 Reading *stramentis* with *Concordia* for *instrumentis*.

all may be in common for them, as it is written.[3] Hence, this same custodian should take the utmost care in choosing garments and distributing the suitable ones, as has been said. No one shall complain when he sees others' garments distributed to him to wear. The awls, needles, and various threads for stitching, mending, or patching the garments are to be distributed by the abbot. Monks should have the opportunity to wash and mend garments when necessary. When new garments are provided, any old clothing, shoes, or bed-covers are to be distributed to the poor by the abbot.

Chapter 5

When the monks gather for their meal at the ninth hour, after reciting a Psalm, one shall read in the center of the hall while the others sit. There shall be no commotion over the food, no one is to talk while eating. If anything is lacking at the table, the one who is in charge may ask by a sign or a silent nod and indicate to the server what must be brought in or what taken from the table. A prayer shall precede their coming to the table. A prayer shall follow their rising from the table and no one shall presume to go anywhere until he shall have given thanks to Christ at the altar. No one is permitted to eat or even to taste meat, not that we consider the creature of God unworthy, but that abstinence from meat is deemed useful and proper for monks. The necessities of the ill and the demands of those going on a long journey are such that the infirm and travelers may eat fowl, provided they observe the moderation befitting piety. If they are entertained by a prince or a bishop, for the sake of blessing and obedience, they need not fear to eat meat, always observing their customary continence the rest of the time. If any monk violates this order and presumes to eat meat against the sanction of

---

3 Cf. Acts 4.32.

the Rule and against ancient custom, he shall be subject to confinement to his cell and penance for the space of six months. For monks are to live on vegetables and greens alone and beans, and rarely on fresh or salt fish, and, then, only when the hospitality shown to guests or the festivity of some holy day makes it possible, always in these and similar cases following the orders of their superior. Each day wine is to be apportioned for drink, but let this sparing use of drink be controlled through the foresight of the abbot or prior—in such wise that one pint may be divided among four brothers. On Saturday and Sunday at *Vespers,* the portion may be increased by one.[1] None of the monks may dare to break his fast, either before they assemble with the rest or after they have eaten, by tasting or touching anything to eat or to drink, nor shall he secretly hide or possess anything of his own. On special solemn occasions, three meals each with food and drink may be offered to the brothers.

Chapter 6

The following methods are to be observed at work. In spring or summer, after reciting *Prime,* the senior monks are to be advised by the prior what work to undertake and they are to inform the rest of the brothers. Then, when the signal is given, they are to take their tools and gather together and say a prayer and go forth to their labor with recitations [of Psalms] until the third hour of the day. Then, returning to the church, after celebrating *Terce,* they are to sit in their places and give attention to reading or prayer. But if the work is such that it cannot be interrupted, then, *Terce* may be recited during the work and so, with recitations, they are to return to their cells and to gather immediately into the church after praying and washing their hands. And if they

---

1 Perhaps one pint for each three men.

are to eat at the sixth hour, after the office of *Sext,* they are to go from prayer to the tables. When sufficiently refreshed, they are to pray again, then become quiet, and there shall be silence until the ninth hour. Then, after reciting *None,* they go back to work if necessary until they reassemble at the appointed office of *Duodecima;* or if those whose age is now advanced are sitting silently in their cells and with pure thoughts meditating silently on the words of God or are carrying out some appointed task within their cells, they are not to go outside except in case of necessity and then only if permitted by their elder. The younger monks sitting next to their deans shall pay attention to the reading or recitation, nor shall any younger monk leave his sitting place without the consent of an elder, nor shall he dare go to the place of another dean, but, both in seclusion and at work, each dean's group shall be separated from another. Each dean shall constantly warn the younger ones in his charge not to fall into idleness and shall always hold up spiritual and holy men as examples to them, so that by contemplating such, they may continuously improve. In autumn and winter they are to read until *Terce* and work until *None,* if there is any work to be done. After *None* again they shall read until *Duodecima,* and then meditate from *Duodecima* until *Vespers.* When they start for work they are to assemble for prayers and when this is over the prior shall commence a Psalm and thus, with recitation, they shall go to their labors. While they work they are not to exchange stories or pleasantries or jokes, but as they work they shall quietly meditate each to himself. While resting they should repeat a Psalm or recite together, or at least be silent. It is a very special precept that no monk shall work as if producing something for himself and no one shall presume to have anything distributed to him just because he wants it. Nor is any work to be undertaken, begun, or completed without the order of an elder or without his consent,[1] but, in every

---

1 Reading *coniventia* with *Concordia* for *cohibentia.*

task, whatever the abbot or prior commands must be done.

Chapter 7

All the tools and utensils of the workmen are to be kept in a single room under the charge of an industrious and understanding brother who will put each tool in its own place as occasion demands and will distribute them to the brothers when they need them for work, and who at *Vespers* will return each to its own place and take care that none of them be lost or allowed to rust through negligence or to be made useless in any other way.

Chapter 8

When the brothers are free from work,[1] none shall dare to leave his place without the permission of his dean or prior, nor to gossip, nor to go on restless, idle walks; but each monk must remain intent upon manual labor or reading or be immersed in the contemplation of prayer until he shall rise when warned by the common signal to share in common prayer or work. At other times, none of the brothers is allowed to look at or speak to another without the permission of his elder. In the dress and walk of a monk, it is established that there shall be no lack of conformity, but the manner of wearing clothes shall remain simple and standard without variation. When they walk, they shall make no noise nor take long steps with outstretched gait. While walking they shall look nowhere except straight ahead on the ground; while talking they shall use a calm low voice without oaths or lies, not searching for guile nor fond of excessive speech, com-

---

1 The word *sessio,* found only in the title of this chapter, means literally "sitting place" or "period for sitting down," normally "leisure," which would hardly seem appropriate here.

pletely free of complaint and altercation and bitterness, hesitant either to condemn another or to judge him free from guilt. Obedience is a precept of the Rule and must be shown by deed and thought, even in impossible matters, and must be persisted in even unto death, *viz:* just as Christ was obedient to the Father even to death.[2] With similar zeal must one observe the virtue of patience, which must never be spoiled by hatred, nor slighted through injury or dishonorable deeds, but strengthened by support and tolerance. Poverty[3] is to be sustained by scarcity of food and hardness of beds. Individual differences in utensils or in clothes or in any matter, even the lowest and most abject, are to be completely avoided. For it is an abomination and a disgrace to monks to possess anything unnecessary, to make anything one's own, or to hide anything, for that is not far different from the example of Ananias and Saphira.[4] No monk is to accept any presents or to receive letters; nor shall he go anywhere without the permission of his elder; nor shall he talk with a layman nor stand and converse with another monk; nor look at anyone else whether a neighbor or a stranger—this is determined by the precepts of the Rule. Nor shall any monk break his fast, nor shall he partake of anything in the nature of food or drink, either before the rest have assembled or after they have eaten with the others—this is commanded by long-standing custom.

Chapter 9

Those chosen for the special weekly duties shall perform their tasks through their particular week, receiving the prayer and benediction of the abbot in the church. On Saturday, when they go out after *Vespers* and all the rest of the brothers have congregated and are sitting in meditation, they shall,

---

2 Cf. Phil. 2.8.
3 Reading *nuditas* with *Concordia* for *ruditas*.
4 Cf. Acts 5.1-11.

with their own hands, wash the feet of each brother with warm water, some washing and some wiping with a towel, and thus, prostrate before the abbot in the same assembly, they shall ask for general forgiveness and blessing from all; and thus commended in the prayer of the abbot, they shall go forth to perform their services for the brothers. In the church the next morning, they shall receive the fullest blessing for their labors.

Chapter 10

With the greatest devotion of love and service are attentions to be bestowed on brothers who are guests or travelers and at *Vespers* their feet are to be washed, and if they are tired from a journey, they should be anointed with oil. Beds, lamps, and soft mattresses are to be provided, and when they leave, they are to have traveling expenses within the means of the monastery. The sick are to be nourished with all care and compassion, and their pains are to be relieved by the proper attentions. Suitable attendants are to be provided to make careful preparation of food and to aid them with loving concern; and no one shall steal from their possessions or make himself guilty of eating forbidden food.

Chapter 11

No one shall take the hand of another or depart at any time without a blessing. Showiness and beauty of garments, elegance, and display of temporal things must be completely avoided by every monk. Vainglory, pride, pompous contempt, and the use of uncontrolled language shall be shunned by all, for the attitude of a monk should be pious, agreeable, humble, and modest. He must be free from all uncleanliness and he should inspire the love and fear of God in all who see or hear him, that it may be fulfilled as the Lord said: "Even so let your light shine before men, in order that they may see your good works and give glory to your Father in heaven."[1]

Chapter 12

Caution and moderation and modesty, faith and sincerity adorn the habit of a monk. The servant of Christ must never be deceitful, but truthful and straightforward and humble of countenance, without any appearance of display. No one shall walk ahead in the company of his elder, or sit down or speak unbidden; but rather must he show proper honor and reverence to his elder brother, as is befitting.

Chapter 13

A monk must always refer to his superior all his deeds and the necessities of every occasion and must guide his actions by his superior's decision and opinion. None shall conceal his thoughts, his visions, his dreams, and his own negligences from an elder, nor the occasions when he is moved by shame or the desire to harm or his being driven by stubbornness. But faults of this sort must be revealed to the abbot, prior, or approved elders, with tears and genuine compunction of the heart and the utmost humility, and they are to be corrected by encouragement, prayer, punishment, or even the imposition of a suitable task.

Chapter 14

When anyone is excommunicated or accused on account of his own negligence, he shall show humility until he receives

1 Matt. 5.16.

reconciliation, nor shall he dare to mingle with others or to meet anyone secretly; but when all have assembled to hear the case, he shall prostrate himself on the ground, throw aside his cincture and outer garment, and ask pardon for his faults. He shall do the same when they return from the divine office. Likewise, also at meal time, he shall stand by the door of the refectory with downcast mien and countenance until, consoled by the compassion of the brothers, he shall receive the pardon which he asks. No one shall speak to an excommunicate nor comfort him with any kind of compassion or pity; nor shall anyone presume to give comfort or to arouse in him the spirit of contradiction and pride. Every case is to be heard in a common assembly of the brothers, and just and careful consideration must be given that an innocent younger brother shall not be oppressed by the craft and malice of an elder. An abbot or prior may not judge by "respect of persons"[1] nor may he fraudulently or unjustly condemn; but, as has been said, the opinion of spiritual and truthful brethren must be followed in matters of this kind. They will set the judgment of God before their eyes and not allow the soul of an innocent man to be unjustly overcome.

Chapter 15

It is unfitting for a monk to be noisy in speech, or wrathful, jesting, or mocking. One who is such and is not corrected, though often chided, must be cured by whipping and beating and must be strongly corrected and must be delivered of his vice by repeated examination and diligence. One who is licentious, quarrelsome, and proud must often be deprived of meals, and often mortified by complete fasts of two or three days, and be further discouraged by the imposition of hard labor; he must be chided with speeches and lectures. If thus

---

1 Cf. 2 Par. 19.7.

punished frequently he still does not change, he must be punished more severely with blows and forced by the deprivation of the divine office and, for a time, nourished only on very small amounts of bread and water, until he promises that he will do no more wrong. The same principles apply to a monk who is disobedient and complaining, contradicting, or given to secret eating and drinking. In all the excesses of the monks a suitable punishment must be applied according to the judgment of the abbot and the elders, giving attention to the type of fault, the age and character of the individual; it must be most diligently seen to that heavy punishment is not inflicted for lesser faults, or, on the other hand, that light and inconsequential punishment declared for the most serious offenses. The head of the abbey and his prior must be continually known for ability to judge and weigh actions, for the sake of pious justice and commiseration, just as one takes care of the wound of a sick person in such a way as to cure rather than damage the injured member; for, just as priors judge the faults of those in their charge, so also will their wrongs be judged by God Himself.

Chapter 16

Monks who lie, steal, strike, or swear falsely in a manner not fitting a servant of Christ must first be verbally chided by their elders to withdraw from their vice. Then, if one has not yet reformed, he shall be brought three times before the brothers and warned to desist completely. If he still does not change, he shall be severely flogged and shall be secluded in a cell under the rigors of penance, having been sentenced to excommunication for three months; he is to be fed six ounces of barley bread each evening and allowed a small measure of water. Anyone found drunk in the monastery shall also be subject to the aforementioned sentence; likewise, any who write letters or receive them from others without the permission of the abbot or prior. A monk who is too attentive to boys or young men or has been caught kissing or indulging in other indiscreet acts, after the case has been openly proved by truthful accusers and witnesses, shall be publicly thrashed; he shall lose the crown which he wears and with head shaven shall be exposed to shame and disgrace; all shall spit in his face and heap their accusations upon him; he shall be bound in iron chains and held in narrow confinement for six months; and shall be given a small amount of barley bread in the evening on three days of each week. After this time is past, for the next six months he shall live in a separate cell under the watchfulness of a spiritual elder and shall be content with manual labor and continual prayer; he shall seek pardon by vigils and tears and abject humility and penitential laments. He shall walk in the monastery under the constant care and watch of two spiritual brothers, and shall never thereafter join the young in private conversation or companionship.

Chapter 17

Any brother who is censured for any negligence or any misconduct, or is excommunicated, and yet humbly seeks pardon or makes tearful confession shall be offered the suitable remedy of forgiveness and indulgence; but the one who is stubborn and unrelenting and proudly or obstinately denying shall receive fuller and more severe punishment and flogging. Two shall not lie in one bed, nor shall anyone be permitted to sleep outside of his own bed. A space of one cubit shall separate each bed, lest incentives of lust be aroused by closeness of bodies. While it is dark, no one shall speak to another, and after *Compline,* no younger monk shall approach the bed of another. The abbot or prior shall change bed assignments twice a week and shall carefully watch to see that no one possesses anything unnecessary or hidden. The night hours must be spent for the most part in special prayers and sacred vigils because of the evil spirits which avoid the light and deceive the servants of God. If a thorn sticks in one's body, none may remove it without the blessing of his elder; none may cut his nails without a blessing; none may lift down from his neck a bundle of any weight whatsoever without the blessing and permission of his elder.

Chapter 18

In fasts, it is necessary to follow this schedule: from Easter to Pentecost, the meal comes at the sixth hour and the custom of eating one meal only is to be observed every day. From Pentecost to September 14, fast is observed every other day[1] except for the 40 days preceding the Feast of Sts. Justus and Pastor[2] when it is to be carefully maintained, and, during this time, the fast must last until the ninth hour each day and wine must be completely avoided. It is within the discretion of the abbot that, if the monks are working very hard, he may give them single portions [of wine] at meal time.[3] From September 14 to Easter, strict fast is enjoined and, during Lent, wine and oil are completely forbidden. If anyone comes to the table late, he shall not be permitted to eat. No one shall enter the oratory for prayer with the rest if he has not arrived by the first Psalm, but he shall be subject to penance. The same penalty is prescribed for one who arrives later than the third Psalm at nightly prayers or tries to stand in the choir after three Psalms have been sung.

---

1 In Isidore, *Regula Monachorum* 11.1, a fast *interdianum* from Lent until the autumnal equinox is clearly in contrast to a fast *cotidianum* during Lent. Elsewhere, *interdianum* means daily.

2 The patron saints of the monastery were two boys who had been martyred under Dacian; their feast fell on Aug. 6.

3 Reading *potiones* with *Concordia* for *portiones*.

Chapter 19

The servants and the prior shall eat with the brothers and shall not presume to prepare special food for themselves, nor eat anything outside of the common meal. The abbot, too, shall try to do this when he is not hindered by guests or by the arrival of a son of the Church. The abbot or prior may not contaminate the brothers by offering food secretly whenever they wish, but only openly when someone is weary from illness or persistent weakness, in which case he shall, with the consent of the rest, publicly order a suitable repast in keeping with age or condition of health.

Chapter 20

Monks may not wander from their duties as they will, unless they get the permission of the prior or senior monk. When necessity requires they may go out accompanied by an elder chosen for this purpose. Abbots or priors shall always be present at divine offices and watches and they shall first perform what they are teaching the rest. An abbot or prior shall always be chosen from the monks of his own monastery— a holy man, discrete, grave, chaste, loving, humble, gentle, and learned, who has been well trained in the aforementioned duties and has had long teaching experience. He should excel in abstinence, be resplendent in learning, have thorough contempt for the fine foods and customs of elegant tables, reject the taking of too much wine, and look after the interests of all the brothers in common, like one's own father in piety. He should not be subject to sudden and immoderate anger, nor lifted by pride, nor broken by sorrow and weakness of spirit, nor corrupted by lust. He must show patience in his decisions, gentleness in his anger, must be so attentive to the poor and needy that he makes himself a servant "in the heart

of Christ,"[1] and not merely a prelate. His speech and manner
of action must be so much alike that he shall strengthen by
zealous deed what he teaches in words, and, advancing[2] with a
two-edged sword,[3] he himself performs with constant care
that on which he has given instruction to others, so that his
deeds may not destroy his words. Nor, on the other hand,
should unsuitable words destroy his deeds, but all things
should be as concordant in a prelate as the harmony of strings
of a lyre or zither, which when struck give out a sweetly-
flowing sound, provided they are struck by the pulsating hand
of one who is well trained and plays in tempered and just
order, without haste and confused unevenness. Three times a
week, a general gathering shall be held and the rules of
the Fathers are to be read; a lecture is to be given or a speech
for the correction and edification of the brothers is to be read
by an elder; wrongs are to be corrected; the excommunicated
may be shown pardon; and the stubborn and hard-headed
once again censured.

Chapter 21

One who desires to leave the world, so the decree of the
Fathers teaches, should not be received in a monastery until
he has made trial of himself in works and poverty, in scorn
and derision. For ten days, he must stand by the door of the
monastery devoted to prayer and fasting, patience and humility. Then, for one full year in the charge of a spiritual
elder, he may not immediately mingle with the congregation,
nor approach the inner[1] habitations of the brothers, but shall
have a special small cell in the outer court, where he shall

1 Phil. 1.8.
2 Reading *praecedens* and observing the punctuation of *Concordia*.
3 Cf. Ps. 56.5.

1 Adopting Ménard's emendation of *interna* for *integra*.

sincerely perform deeds of obedience. He shall carry the beddings for guests and travelers, warm the water for their feet, and perform all services humbly, and shall daily carry on his back a bundle of wood for the use of the monks on weekly assignments. And so bowed down in every degree of poverty and service, tried in character for a full year, and purified with labor, he shall receive the blessing of the Church and be united with the society of the brothers and shall be assigned to a dean to be instructed in the performance of every good deed. If any candidate, however, is outstanding for goodness and purity of life and is approved in the opinion of the abbot and the other spiritual brothers, he may in a shorter time join the congregation of the brothers in return for the merit and purity of his conscience, according to whatever decision may be made in the deliberations of the abbot or the more trustworthy brothers.

Chapter 22

Every candidate, when he comes to the monastery to be received, shall be immediately brought before the whole congregation and interrogated by the abbot as to his status, whether free or slave, whether he wishes in good faith and free will to be admitted, or from some compulsion and necessity. When his desire for the religious life seems spontaneous and he appears not to be subject to any bonds or conditions, the abbot shall receive his oath,[1] which contains the complete foundation of his religious profession, and by which the candidate shall bind himself to fulfill faithfully all the laws and customs of the monastery and never to act against them, and shall promise never to depart from the strict observance of the rule of the monastery which he is seeking to join. When

---

1 Herwegen (65-70) shows that this *pactum* cannot be the well-known one, because the candidate has not been there one year. He gives an example of a candidate's oath.

he has bound himself by this profession, he is to be subject to the aforementioned rules, seeking always to please God by the diligent performance of good deeds.

Chapter 23

The monk who was the first of those in the monastery to be professed shall be the first to walk, the first to sit, the first to receive the benediction, the first to take communion in the church, the first to speak when the brothers are asked about some matter, the first to recite the Psalm, the first to stand in the choir, the first to perform the weekly assignments, and the first to extend his hand at table. It is not age alone that is to be taken as a criterion among the brothers, but the date of profession and the conduct of work and study. Hence, this distinction is to be paid to an elder to honor him according to the degree of his fervent love and worship of God. It is not dignity of birth, nor the wealth of possessions that one had in the world, nor advance of age that is to be considered, but uprightness of life and the rewards merited by an ardent faith are to be weighed. He must be judged the stronger who is closer to God. Monks must continue to live a holy, chaste, and honorable life within the monastery; laymen may carry out the orders of an abbot or prior outside the institution.[1] Monks may not leave the monastery without the permission of the abbot or prior, and they must not leave the seclusion of their own cells, except, of course, to go to the nearby garden or orchard with the blessing of an elder; but

---

1 The text ends here in all the manuscripts, but a little of the lost material has been recovered by Martins and printed in *O monacato de san Frutuoso de Braga* 404-05. Martins found the text for the last two sentences of chapter 23 and a surviving sentence of chapter 24 in Madrid, Bibl. Nac. 13085, which otherwise has a total of only 21 chapters in a completely different order. Chapter 25 should have referred, according to the title in the Contents, to Sunday observances in the monastery, but the Latin of the text is not found in any manuscript presently known.

it is not permitted to visit the surrounding villages or farms or any secular possessions. If anyone tries to do so, he shall be subject to excommunication and penance for two months and shall subsist on a small amount of bread and water.

Chapter 24

Brothers who have grown old living a good and pious life in the monastery may have servants appointed by the abbot and may be assigned large separate cells, where a meal may be prepared and a table set for them, both at *Sext* and at *Vespers*, because of their weakness and the advent of old age.

GENERAL RULE FOR MONASTERIES

(*Regula Monastica Communis*)

CONTENTS

Chapter 1

Some are accustomed for fear of Gehenna to found monasteries within their own homes, and to join in common under
the terms of an oath with their wives and children and

slaves and neighbors, and, as we have said, to consecrate for
themselves churches on their own estates, name these after
the martyrs, and falsely to call such establishments monasteries. We consider these not monasteries, but the perdition
of souls and the subversion of the Church. From such have
arisen heresy and schism and great controversy throughout
the monasteries. Heresy [Greek "choice"] is so named because each one chooses what he prefers to do; his choice he
considers sacred and he defends it with lying words. When
you find any such, you should consider them hypocrites and
heretics rather than monks. We hope and most earnestly
beseech your holy reverence that you will not hold converse
with such, nor imitate them. Because they live by their own
rules, they want to be subject to none of the elders and they
donate none of their own possessions to the poor. On the
contrary, they try to seize from others so that, with their wives
and children, they may make greater profit than when they
were in the world. In so doing, they show no concern for
the perdition of their souls, so that they reap the advantages,
not of their souls, but of their bodies, and that even more so
than men of the world. They grieve for their precious possessions like wolves, and from day to day they sorrow over
wrongs unavenged. Scandalously they pant with passion for
gain and care not for future punishment, being too keenly
preoccupied with feeding their wives and children. In the heat
of grievous quarrels and disagreements they break off with
those neighbors to whom they had previously been bound by
oaths, and they attempt to seize from each other the property
that previously they had pooled and managed in fictitious
charity. If they detect any weakness in some of the community,
they seek the aid of the relatives they left in the world, with
their swords and clubs and threats, and at the very beginning
of their life in religion plot to upset everything around them.
Since they are vulgar and ignorant, they want their abbot
to be the same, so that wherever they desire to turn, they may

perform all their own wishes with his blessing, and may say anything they want to say, and may judge others as though conducting an investigation, and may tear apart the servants of Christ with the teeth of dogs. All this they do that they may have common consort with the people and with the princes of this world and with the world may love the world. May they perish with the world, unclean as they are.[1] They often invite others to live in the same way, and prepare an obstacle for their weak minds. Of such, the Lord says in the Gospel: "Beware of false prophets, who come to you in sheep's clothing, but inwardly are ravenous wolves. By their fruits you will know them . . . nor can a bad tree bear good fruit."[2] By their fruits, he means their works; by their leaves, their words. So that you may know them in their works, you can weigh their words; for, when they are lighted by the torch of cupidity, they cannot rival the poor of Christ. It is customary for the poor in Christ to desire nothing in this world, that they may perfectly love God and their neighbor. In order to escape the aforementioned wolves, they have listened to the word of the Lord, saying: "Behold, I am sending you forth like sheep in the midst of the wolves";[3] "you shall not carry purse nor wallet."[4] Accordingly, the servant of Christ who desires to be a true disciple will, stripped of all, climb the naked cross, that he may be dead to the world, but alive in the crucified Christ. And after he has laid down the burden of his body and seen the enemy slain, then, will he think that he has conquered the world and won a triumph equal with that of the holy martyrs.

---

1 Pun on *mundus* and *immundi*.
2 Matt. 7.15, 16, 18.
3 Matt. 10.16.
4 Luke 10.4.

Chapter 2

Some presbyters are wont to simulate sanctity, not for
eternal life, but to serve the Church for love of worldly goods;
and under the prctcxt of sanctity, to pursue the emoluments
of riches. And they attempt to build so called monasteries,
not because they have been stirred by the love of Christ, but
under the enticements of the common crowds, in fear of
losing their titles or giving up their other rewards. This they
do, not after the manner of the apostles, but in the way of
Ananias and Saphira.[1] Of these the blessed Jerome said:[2]
"They have not distributed their goods to the poor, nor
have they lived a laborious life of exercise in the monastery;
they have not watched over their way of living to correct it
by constant meditation. They have not wept, they have not
rolled their bodies in ashes and wrapped themselves in sackcloth;[3] they have not preached penitence to sinners that they
might say with John the Baptist: 'Repent, for the kingdom
of heaven is at hand.'[4] They have not imitated Christ who
said: 'I did not come to be ministered unto but to minister,'[5]
and: 'I have come not to be served, but to serve my Father.' "[6]
And when such men are brought from one rank to another—
I mean on account of their pride—they want to be in charge
of the brothers, not to act for their interest; and while
greedily[7] hanging on to what they have, they begin to desire
what others have, just because they do not share it; and they
preach what they do not themselves practice; and they keep
a common Rule with bishops and secular princes of the
earth and the people, and, like the disciples of Antichrist
which they are, they bark against the Church; and they
construct battering rams with which to attack the Church;

---

1 Cf. Acts 5.1-11.
2 Unidentified.
3 Cf. Matt. 11.21.
4 Matt. 3.2.
5 Cf. Matt. 20.28.
6 Cf. John 6.38.

yet when they come into our midst with lowered head and
well-paced step they pretend sanctity. These are hypocrites,
who are one thing, but appear to be another, so that the
fools who see them imitate them. They are thieves and robbers, who, in the words of the Lord,[8] enter not by the door,
which is Christ, but by breaking through the wall of the
Church and rushing in; and if any of the faithful desires to
live rightly, they will set up obstacles against such, as best
they can, rather than aid them. Of such the Lord said:
"Woe to you, Scribes and Pharisees, blind hypocrites! because you shut the kingdom of heaven and you yourselves
do not enter in, nor permit others to enter."[9] Such are delighted both with their own gains and with our losses; and
if they have not heard anything false to bring against us, with
all haste they make it up, and though we know we did not
do it criminals go up and down the streets reporting it against
us, and then they defend them; those whom we drive out of
the monastery for their sins are by them received with an
ovation, protected, and defended; and although most of our
detractors are deserters of monasteries, they honor them
highly and—shame to say—heap dignities upon them. When
you see such as these, it is better to show them hatred than
companionship, for of such the prophet said: "Do I not hate,
O Lord, those who hate you? . . . With a deadly hatred I
hate them; they are my enemies."[10]

Chapter 3

First of all, an abbot must be sought who is seasoned by
the practices of a holy life; not one who is newly professed,
but who, for a long period of time, has been proved by labor-

---

7 Reading *tumide* for *timide*.
8 Cf. John 10.1, 2.
9 Cf. Matt. 23.13.
10 Ps. 138.21, 22.

ing hard in a monastery under an abbot in the company
of many, who does not have an inheritance in the world, but
is a true Levite in all Israel without a share in the land of
promise, so that he may freely say with the prophet: "The
Lord is my inheritance";[1] to such a degree that he banishes
completely from his heart all use of litigation, and, if there
be a question of rights, does not contend with men in court
under any circumstances; but, if anyone incites him and takes
away his tunic to make him fight, straightway, in accordance
with the word of the Lord, he lets him have his cloak as well.[2]
If some complainant comes to bother the monastery and to
take something away from it and even uses violence in so
doing, the abbot should turn the matter over to a layman,
himself a most faithful Christian, commended for his good life
and not tainted by evil report, who without sin shall judge
and inquire about the affairs of the monastery; and if there
is need of oath, he shall administer it without swearing and
the penalty of swearing; and he shall proceed in such a way
as to see not only to the interest of the monastery but to make
the persecutor humble and inclined to ask forgiveness. But,
if the complainant continues stubbornly in his unheeding
ways and loves gain more than his soul, then, the pleader shall
immediately drop the case. An abbot should live a simple
life in his monastery with his monks, not trying to cause
quarrels but swallowing all bitterness and finding no cause
for litigation with men in the world.

Chapter 4

Monks who seek to enter the monastery by profession of
religion shall, first, live outside the gates for three days and
nights and shall be continually reproved by the monks assigned each week. After this time they shall be asked whether

---

1 Cf. Ps. 15.5.
2 Cf. Matt. 5.40.

they are free or slaves. If they are slaves, they may not be received unless they bring with them proof that freedom has been granted by their own masters; as for the rest, whether free or slaves, rich or poor, married or single, foolish or wise, unskilled or trained, young or old, whatever they are, they must be carefully questioned as to whether their profession is proper or not; whether they have done everything which they have heard in the words of Verity in the Gospel, which says: "Who has not renounced all that he possesses cannot be my disciple";[1] and the case of the rich young man who boasted that he had fulfilled all the commands of the law, to whom the Lord said: "If thou wilt be perfect, go sell what thou hast, and give to the poor, and come, follow me and thou shalt have treasure in heaven."[2] Again the Lord said to him: "Who wishes to be perfect? Who like the apostles leaves his father and mother, his nets and boat."[3] He who said, "all" had nothing reserved for his own use, but gave his possessions, not to a particular person, but to the poor in Christ; and gave not to his father, not to his mother, not to his brother, not to his neighbor, not to his relations, not to his adoptive child, not to his wife, not to his children, not to the Church, not to the princes of the earth, not to his servants, except to establish them in freedom. When he has been questioned, as I have said, he may be admitted to the lowest rank. But, if any of these whom we have mentioned shall, according to the usages of piety, renounce falsely and leave so much as a single coin anywhere, we order him to be thrown out immediately, for we see him not in the number of the apostles, but rather a follower of Ananias and Saphira.[4] You should know that he cannot live up to the measure of a monk in a monastery, nor stoop to the poverty of Christ, nor acquire humility, nor be obedient, nor abide there continuously;

---

1 Cf. Luke 14.26, 27.
2 Matt. 19.21.
3 Cf. Matt. 4.20-22.
4 Cf. Acts 5.1-11.

but, when some occasion arises for him to be reprimanded or corrected by the abbot of his monastery for any cause, he will straightway allow his pride to overcome him, will be inflated with weakness of spirit, and will flee and leave the monastery behind him.

Chapter 5

Monks should obey the commands of their elders as Christ was obedient to the Father, even to death; if they do otherwise, they should know that they have lost the way which they were seeking. No one goes to Christ except through Christ. Accordingly monks should adopt such ways that they may not in any wise deviate from the true path. First of all they must learn to conquer their own desires, and not to do anything even of the smallest import of their own will, not to say anything unless asked, to drive out with fasting and prayer the thoughts that arise from day to day, and to conceal nothing from their abbot. And whatever they do they must do without complaint, lest—and may this never happen—by their complaints, they perish like those who perished in the desert.[1] Those complainers in the desert perished by eating manna, while these in the monastery die daily mouthing the scriptures. Those because of their complaints did not enter the land of promise, and these because of their complaints do not enter the land of promise of Paradise. What a terrible loss to leave Egypt, to have crossed the sea, to have played upon the tambourine with Moses and Mariam when Pharao drowned,[2] to have eaten manna and yet not to have entered the land of promise; how much greater a misfortune to leave the Egypt of this world, to pass daily through the sea of baptism with the bitterness of penitence, to beat upon the drum, that is, to

1 Cf. Num. 11, 14, 16, 20.
2 Cf. Exod. 15.20.

crucify the flesh with Christ, and to eat the manna which is heavenly grace, and yet not to enter the land of the heavenly kingdom. You must fear, then, dearest brothers, and think and meditate in advance on what way men should follow who wish to go through Christ to Christ; they must listen clearly to what they must observe. They shall be obedient to the abbot to death to such an extent that they may not do their own will, but that of the Father.[3] Nothing is so dear to God as when we crush our own wills. Hence, Peter said: "We have left all and followed thee; what then shall we have?"[4] He said not only: "We have left all; what then shall we have?", but added: "We have followed thee." Many give up everything, but do not follow the Lord. Why? because they follow their own desire, not that of the Father. Who, therefore, wishes to find the straight and narrow path and to continue upon it without stumbling and wishes not to lose his way while proceeding and to reach Christ without losing his way must, first, learn to overcome his own desires and to do none of the things which his own bodily desires wish to do and to persevere to the end of life in obedience to the Father. Such is the straight and narrow path that leads to life.

Chapter 6

When someone comes with his wife and small children—children under the age of seven, that is—it is in keeping with the holy General Rule that both the parents and the children may be received under the power of the abbot, who shall explain to them, understandably and with due concern, what rules they must observe. First of all, they may have no power over their own persons nor take thought for food or clothing; nor shall they presume to keep in their possession any longer

---

3 Cf. John 6.38.
4 Matt. 19.27.

the wealth and lands which they have left, but they shall
live as guests and travelers subject to the monastery; the
parents shall not be anxious for their children, nor the
children for their parents. They may not hold converse together, except with the permission of the prior. As for the
tiniest children, however, who are still in the cradle, for the
sake of due compassion, they may go to their father or mother
when they wish, lest the parents fall into the vice of making
complaints for them, which often gets to be a serious problem
in a monastery. Let the children be brought up by both
parents until they come to know a little about the Rule;
and let them be instructed continually so that both boys and
girls may be trained in the way of life of the monastery
where they are going to live. And now, if God grants us
opportunity, we are going to show fully how the children are
to be fed in the monastery. An attendant (*cellarius*) is to be
chosen, tried for his patience, elected by the common assembly,
excused from all monastery service and kitchen duties, who
will always watch over the chamber reserved for infants,
the aged, the sick, and guests. And if the congregation is
sufficiently large, a younger monk may be given to him to aid
in hastening about his duties, so that the small children may
be brought together under his direction and given their food
at suitable hours. From holy Easter to September 24, they
may eat four times a day; from September 24 to December 1,
three times; and from December 1 to holy Easter, the matter
shall be under the direction of the attendant himself. But the
children are to be instructed that they may put nothing in
their mouths without a blessing and permission; and the
children shall each have their superior (*decanus*) who knows
more about them and watches the observance of the Rule
over them; and they are to be taught by him not to do or say
anything except in accordance with the Rule; and not to be
caught lying, stealing, and swearing falsely. If they shall
be caught in one of these faults, they are to be corrected by

their dean immediately with a whip. The attendant himself shall wash their feet and clothes and teach them with all due attention how to advance in holiness, that he may receive the full reward from the Lord and may hear the words of Verity who said: "Let the little children be, and do not hinder them from coming to me, for of such is the kingdom of heaven."[1]

Chapter 7

Those who are ill from any disease may lie in a single room and be assigned to the care of someone suitable; and they shall receive such attendance that they shall not crave the love of their relatives nor the enticements of worldly goods, but let the attendant and prior provide everything necessary. The ill, however, are to be warned by this solicitous care that not even so much as a whisper of complaint may come from their mouths, but that they should always offer thanks to God in their illness with steadfast mien, without interruption, without any exhibition of complaint, and with true compunction of heart, and they shall in no way dare to offend the brother who is ministering to them.[1] But if some scruple of complaint should come from their mouths, as I have said, they are to be chided by the abbot and warned not to do any of the aforementioned things, in such a way that the one upon whom this service is enjoined shall be the one to charge them.

Chapter 8

Some old novices regularly come to the monastery and we know that many of them promise observance of the rule out of

---

1 Matt. 19.14.

---

1 Changing *audeat* to *audeant* with Ménard and also *frater* to *fratrem*; but *frater* may be a colloquialism (hanging nominative).

want and weakness and not to profess the religious life.
When such are found, they must be investigated very carefully, and amid the other legal questionings they are to answer
only what is asked. For they have a way of never giving up
their previous customs and of wandering into idle tales, as
they were long trained. When they are corrected by some
spiritual brother, they immediately burst into anger and, for
a long time, they are urged on by the ills of spiritual weakness
and they never completely cease from rancor and bitterness.
And when they slip into such faults, so often and so extensively, when even their spiritual weakness leaves them, they
usually loose their restraint to the extent of the telling
of idle stories and in laughter. Accordingly, they are to be
introduced to the monastery with this precaution, that they
are not to tell idle stories day or night, but are to give themselves to sobs and tears, to ashes and sackcloth, and are with
throbbing hearts to do penance for their past sins and
not again to commit acts that require penance. The degree of
pravity which they previously devoted to sin must be doubled
in the full devotion paid to lamentation. Since for seventy
and more years they have so abundantly sinned, it is fitting
that they be bound in severe penance, just as a surgeon cuts
into a wound more deeply when he sees rotten flesh. Such are
to be corrected by true penance; if they are unwilling, then,
they are to be punished immediately with excommunication.
If they have been warned twice seven times and have not
given up this vice, they are to be brought to an assembly of
elders and there, for the last time, are to be examined. If they
do not permit themselves to amend their ways, they must be
dismissed. On the other hand, we may show mercy to them as
to little children; we may honor them as fathers, if they are
quiet, simple, humble, obedient, frequently in prayer, deploring their own sins as much as those of others, daily risking
their lives, always keeping Christ on their lips, not being idle
when they have strength to work, guided by the opinion of

their elders rather than by their own, completely abandoning all family affection, giving all they have to Christ's poor rather than to their relatives, keeping nothing for themselves, with all their mind and courage observing the law of God and their neighbors, day and night meditating on the law of the Lord. They may be excused from duties in the bakery and kitchen and may be free from working in the field and on heavy jobs, except that some of the lighter tasks may be assigned to them, lest their weary years be completely broken before their time. The food which they eat may be purposely cooked soft and tender by the weekly workers and they may, because of their weakness, have a moderate amount of meat and wine; they shall all come to eat at one table, they shall all have the same food and drink. They may have such clothing and shoes that they can avoid chilling cold without the use of fire.

Chapter 9

Those who accept the charge of attending the livestock of the monastery[1] should show such concern for them that they will not cause any harm to the crops, and they should be watched so carefully and so astutely that they will not be devoured by wild beasts, and they should be kept away from steep and rocky mountains and inaccessible valleys, so that they will not slip over a precipice. But, if any of the above-mentioned negligent deeds happens because of inattention or lack of care on the part of the shepherds, they shall straight-way throw themselves at the feet of their elders and, as though deploring great sins, shall for a considerable time suffer penance worthy of such a fault, after which they shall return and humbly ask forgiveness; or if they are boys, they should be given their correction and punishment with a whip. The flocks are to be placed in the charge of a monk who is well-

---

1 This chapter is peculiar to Galicia; there are no parallels in other *Rules*.

proved, who was trained to this sort of work while in the world, and who desires to guard the flocks with such good intention that never the slightest complaint comes from his lips. They may have younger ones assigned to them by turns to share their labor. They may have sufficient clothing and covering for the feet. One monk, such as we have mentioned, shall be responsible for this service, so as not to inconvenience all the monks in the monastery. But since some who guard the flocks are accustomed to complain and think they have no reward for such service when they cannot be seen praying and working in the congregation, let them harken to the words of the Rules of the Fathers and silently reflect upon them and enjoin such upon themselves, recognizing the examples of the Fathers of old, for the patriarchs tended flocks, and Peter performed the duties of a fisherman, and Joseph the Just, to whom the Virgin Mary was espoused, was a carpenter. Accordingly, they have no reason to dislike the sheep which have been assigned to them, for they shall reap not one but many rewards. Their young shall be refreshed, their old shall be warmed, their captives redeemed, their guests and strangers entertained. Besides, most monasteries would scarcely have enough food for three months, if there existed only the daily bread in this province, which requires more work on the soil than any other land. Therefore, one who is assigned this task should happily obey and should most firmly believe that his obedience frees him from all danger and prepares for him a great reward before God, just as the disobedient one suffers the loss of his soul.

Chapter 10

First of all, abbots must observe the canonical hours, that is, *Prime,* when the workers are sent to the vineyard; *Terce,* when the Holy Spirit descended upon the apostles; *Sext,* when

the Lord ascended onto the Cross; *None,* when He gave up
the Spirit; *Vespers,* when David sang: "The lifting up of my
hands, the evening sacrifice";[1] *Midnight,* because at that hour
a cry arose: "Behold, the bridegroom is coming, go forth
to meet him,"[2] and in order that the hour when He shall
come to judge may find us not sleeping, but watching; *Cockcrow,* when Christ rose from the dead. These canonical hours
the Catholic or universal Church celebrates unceasingly from
the orient to the occident. Accordingly, abbots must celebrate
them in every monastery with full attention, with weeping
and contrition of heart, dismissing all need for labor or travel,
together with the whole congregation of monks. When it shall
be absolutely necessary for them to travel and they know that
the times of these hours have come, they shall straightway
prostrate themselves upon the ground and humbly seek indulgence from the Lord. They need not be hesitant to pray at
their own special hours, that is, the second, fourth, fifth, seventh, eighth, tenth, and eleventh, inasmuch as seven or eight
are harmonious in the words of Solomon: "Make seven or
eight portions,"[3] in order that they may be able to climb
through the sevenfold grace of the Spirit and the eight beati-
tudes on the day[4] of resurrection with unhampered tread up
the ladder of Jacob by its fifteen steps to the region of heaven,
where Christ is resplendent above. Secondly, at the beginning
of each month, abbots in one district shall gather in one place
and solemnly celebrate monthly litanies and implore the aid
of God in behalf of the souls entrusted to them, inasmuch
as they hope to render an account of themselves to God at that
tremendous judgment and mighty inquest. Thirdly, they
shall make rules there for the conduct of their daily life, and
they shall return to their cells chastened, as if reprehended

---

1 Cf. Ps. 140.2.
2 Matt. 25.6.
3 Eccles. 11.2.
4 Reading *die* for *diem.*

by their magistrates.[5] Fourthly, they must inquire into and study the past sayings of the Fathers in their writings, in order to know from them what they should do themselves, so that, inside and out, before and behind, they have a mind full of eyes, lest they fall into some heresy—heaven forbid—and perish. For this, they must always stand in the council of the brothers on balanced scales as though being weighed, that, by recalling the past, foreseeing the future, and examining the present, they may avoid the goads of heresy. Fifthly, abbots are to live at one common table with brothers who are travelers and strangers, because the Lord said of them: "I was a stranger and you took me in."[6] Sixthly, abbots must so conduct themselves as to completely remove all greed and avarice. If this were not an evil, the apostles would not have called it "idolatry."[7] By such poison we know the mind of a monk is wounded; never will he be completely free from all fault who is bound by the chain of such a habit; and he will never be firm in the love of God and of his neighbor, because what we desire in this world we shall doubtless hate in the next. Hence the holy Fathers, filled with the Holy Spirit to love God and their neighbor perfectly, wanted to have nothing in this world, but, because we cannot exist without something, we should possess what will not make us ashamed when we must give to a needy neighbor, and we must never let our souls relax from the love of God and of our neighbor. The strength of such love is praised by the true words of Holy Church when it is said in the Canticle of Canticles: "For stern as death is love."[8] Love is compared to the sternness of death, for, doubtless, once it comes, it summons the mind completely away from the love of the world. Accordingly, abbots must be such that they may perfectly love God and their neighbor; they must have

---

5 Reading *saionibus* with the *Concordia* for *senioribus*.
6 Matt. 25.35.
7 Gal. 5.20.
8 Cant. 8.6.

their eyes removed from the evil desires of this world, as Adam did in Paradise before the fall.

Chapter 11

Priors shall administer all the rules of the monastery. Those elected priors must be like those recognized as abbots, so that they may take care of the onerous tasks of the abbots. Abbots are to make use themselves of the same food and clothing that is administered by them to others, and except when brothers are visiting or in case of illness, abbots are not to eat more choice food, but the same as the brothers. Priors shall have control of dispensing all the possessions of the monastery; if a captive asks the abbot for some food for whatever cause, the prior shall take care of it and shall eagerly and carefully see to it that the abbot shall not have extra work, with the exceptions that we have just mentioned; both the abbot and the prior shall have the power of excommunication. At the beginning of each month, the prior shall give an account to his abbot of all that has been expended during the preceding month, and shall do it with trembling and with a straightforward manner and true humility of heart, as if rendering an account to his Lord. All that he does shall depend upon the judgment of the abbot: he shall presume nothing of his own, lest he fall—heaven forbid—into the disease of vainglory. He should always be a thrifty, not prodigal, dispenser to the household of Christ, a pious and excellent governor, observing the example of the Gospel and the words of the Lord, who said: "Who, dost thou think, is the faithful and prudent servant whom his master has set over his household to give them their food in due time? Blessed is that servant whom his master, when he comes, shall find so doing. Amen I say to you, he will set him over all his goods."[1]

---

1 Matt. 24.45, 46.

Chapter 12

Deans who are set up over their groups of ten should show such concern for the brothers over whom they have been placed that these may never perform their own will. They are not to speak unless questioned; not to do anything of their own accord unless ordered; not to go anywhere unless commanded; are to fear their elders as masters and to love them as parents; are to perform any commands they receive from them; are to consider as salutary any instructions they receive from their elders, provided they are carried out without complaint, good naturedly, and in silence, just as Moses said: "Listen, Israel, and be silent."[1] "Bear one another's burdens."[2] None shall judge another, none shall condemn another, for it is written: "Every detractor shall be wiped out."[3] Each one may take from another the virtue he does not have; each may learn humility from another, each may learn love from another, each may learn patience from another, each may learn silence from another, each may learn compassion from another. Deans are to eat without complaint whatever is placed in front of them, to wear whatever they receive. The brothers are not to hide their daily thoughts from the deans; the deans are to be guides and guardians, as if they would have to render an account to the Lord for the brothers. The deans shall watch for faults on the part of all and shall have the power of correcting them. What they are unable to correct, they must not hesitate to lay before the prior. The priors are to handle such matters so rigorously and so rationally that they will never have to trouble their abbots, except on matters for which neither deans nor priors have been able to reach a quick settlement. In this procedure, each shall have such humility

---

1 Cf. Deut. 27.9.
2 Gal. 6.2.
3 Cf. Matt. 15.13. C. J. Bishko, "The Spanish *Consensoria Monachorum*," *American Journal of Philology* 69 (1948) 379 n., calls this a quotation from an uncanonical prophetic tract.

before the other that he shall never offend another, but each shall stand before the other as though on a balance, that is, the juniors to the deans, the deans to the priors, the priors to the abbots, each one supporting the others like squared blocks in a wall, after the words of the apostle mentioned before: "Bear one another's burdens, and so you will fulfill the law of Christ."[4]

Chapter 13

All the deans shall be advised by their priors that all the brothers from the least to the greatest shall assemble in one place in the monastery on Sundays, so that they may be diligently scrutinized by the abbot before solemn mass, so that none may be goaded by hate and bitterness toward another, or be wounded by the spear of malice; lest internal poison occasionally break out on the surface of the skin and the bitterness of myrrh be shown among the fruits of the palms. First of all, then, the abbots with their priors and deans are to examine one another and, likewise, to question their younger subjects; and, on the aforementioned days, they are to root all traces of malice from their hearts. Some are accustomed under guise of piety to show anxiety for their wives and children or even other relatives. Some who are not so involved become anxious over their food. Others are consumed inwardly with the ills of dejection and are devoured by the anxiety of their minds, just as a garment is inwardly devoured by a moth, and, with the languor of bitterness, they slip into despair. Others are more strongly fired by the spirit of fornication and are often led along like captives, incited by this taunt of the flesh, their interior vision blinded, bound by the chain of perdition. Others, inflated by the spirit of laziness, wish to spend their time resting and sleeping

---

4 Gal. 6.2.

and entertain themselves with curious tales and, what is worse, think of leaving their own monastery. Others are pierced in several places by the spear of vainglory, while others, defending one thing or another, magnifying their own cares, unwilling to be like the poor in Christ, slip each one into those vain thoughts and, as though they had received nothing from God, they extol themselves for their own powers, and when they can find no one else to praise them, they launch into their own praises. One boasts of his family background and that princes came from his line, another boasts of his parents, another of his brothers, another of his relatives, another of his married relations, another of his superior slaves,[1] another of his wealth, another of the flower of his youth, another of his courage in war, another of his travels about the world, another of cleverness, another of wisdom, another of his power of eloquence, another of his silence, another of his humility, another of his love, another of his generosity, another of his chastity, another of his being married, another of his poverty, another of his abstinence, another of the number of public speeches he has delivered, another of his watchfulness, another of his obedience, another of his renunciation of goods, another of his reading, another of his writing, another of his rhythmical voice. By speaking so often immoderately and without permission of all these things that we have enumerated at length, and by lending themselves so often to vainglory, they go from this disease to pride, as they try to prove their claims. For this reason, we order all the brothers to take part in the assembly and not to allow more than seven days between meetings and every Sunday to correct their former customs and faults. Each one must fight against that fault which he has admitted and against which he himself knows there is a struggle. If any matters are brought out by others, the one who is suffering must accept the disclosure without shame.

---

1 *Idoneus* is a technical word in Visigothic law for a better class of slaves. It may also refer to freedmen.

If he does not do the least that is in his power, he may be sure that he is not escaping the devil, and must consider himself not conqueror, but conquered. But if he does confess and does amend through penance or flagellation, he will straightway drive the enemy into a covered trap and bury him.

Chapter 14

When a monk is excommunicated for a crime, he shall be put in a solitary dark cell and fed only on bread and water, so that at *Vespers,* after the brothers have eaten, he may receive half a small loaf of bread and some water, but not to satiety, and this not blessed by the abbot, but exorcised by blowing on it [three times]. He must sit without comfort or conversation from the brothers, unless the abbot or prior has given someone authority to speak to him. The excommunicate must perform the work of the monastery while wearing sackcloth or covering without heavy nap, half-naked and barefoot. If his excommunication is for two days or three days, the superior who excommunicated him shall send one of the well-tried elders to rebuke him with words of reproach, because he did not act in consideration of religion nor for love of Christ, nor for fear of hell, but to cause a disagreement among the faithful brothers. If he patiently endures this and no word of anger or complaint comes from his mouth and his sincerity and humility are apparent, then, the elder sent to reproach him shall without changing any words report to the abbot what he has seen. The abbot shall carefully and prudently consider whether the patience by which the excommunicate may once again win the love of the brothers is true or false. A second time, he shall send to reprove him another elder of the same merit and he shall not easily believe what he heard the first time. When he has done so for a third time, and again chided him in equal degree, and the excommunicate has persisted in the endurance of his former promise, and

the abbot has proved it by three witnesses, then, he shall have
him released and, when brought before him, shall chide him
in the assembly of the brothers. When thus he has been tried
a fourth time and proved in his humility and found as strong
as iron, then, he shall enter the church and take a cincture
in his hands and fall at the feet of the abbot and the brothers
with tears and with sobs and groans; crawling with his knees
on the ground, he shall ask pardon of all and shall be warned
not to commit again deeds worthy of similar penance; then
he shall be restored to his rank by a kiss from the abbot. If,
however, as we have indicated above, an excommunicate appears quarrelsome or complaining during his first investigation
and tries proudly or insistently to vindicate his intentions, and
the elder recognizes this to be the case, he shall remain there
until the third day of his excommunication without anyone
speaking to him. If, when similarly interrogated on the third
day, he is still guilty of the pride which we mentioned, he shall
be confined to the workshop until he successfully denies all his
arrogant pride. If he continues in his evil and does not of his
own accord do penance, and over and over is openly bitter and
complaining to his superior or the brothers in their presence,
and prefers to defend himself with the aid of his relatives, he
must be brought to an assembly, deprived of the vestments
of the monastery, given the secular garments which he once
wore, and expelled from the monastery with the mark of
shame, in order that others may be corrected by his being,
perhaps, the only example of a delinquent needing such
punishment.

Chapter 15

It is in accord with the holy Common Rule that monks shall
not live in one monastery with nuns nor presume to have a
common oratory; in fact, they shall not remain in one common
room or one common building even for the gravest necessity—
no form of excuse being acceptable. Monks who have nuns

in their charge must be certain not to take the license of eating in the same hall or dining room, nor of performing in common labor any ordered task, but, if it happens that one shall be sick, they are each to have separate quarters and good guardians. They shall work in such great silence that neither group shall hear a word uttered by the other, except for recitations and the chanting of liturgical songs, and, of course, each group may sigh and weep among themselves. Such prudence must be taken in this matter as though a night-time thief were trying to kill Christ in our hearts and wanted to choke, not our bodies, but our souls. Therefore we cautiously strengthen this Rule to such an extent that no monk shall converse alone with a nun. If they do so, they must realize that they are breaking the rules of the Fathers and that the arrow of death has penetrated to the center of their hearts. For this the life of Paradise is lost, and to this loss is added the punishment of hell. Believe me, you who are often associated in the company of women cannot wholeheartedly dwell with the Lord. It was through a woman that a serpent, that is, the devil, trapped our first parent, and, because he was obedient to the devil rather than to God, he straightway felt the ills of the flesh, and for this reason we the sons experience the passion through which we know that our parents were deprived of the delights of Paradise. We must therefore watch and constantly pray and with all our strength avoid allowing our senses to be captivated by such enticements. Therefore, a monk alone shall not speak to a nun alone, even though they meet on a journey. No nun may travel alone, but only when accompanied by another nun. If, from among the acts criticized above, a monk alone shall be caught speaking to a nun alone, he shall be publicly stretched out and flogged with one hundred blows of the lash. One who dares to do such a thing shall be threatened and warned that he has violated the laws of the monks; if he repeats the crime a second time, he shall be beaten and then thrown into prison; or if he refuses to repent, he shall be dismissed from the monastery.

Chapter 16

The monks who live in the women's monasteries we order to dwell far from the living quarters. Such monks must be few and perfect, chosen for being approved among many; who have grown old having spent most of their lives in the monastery; who have always been approved by a life of perpetual chastity; and who have never been excommunicated outside the Church for any crimes. Those who live in the women's monasteries must be capable of performing odd jobs[1] for them and must prepare hospitality for visiting brothers, and shall guard the young of both sexes as carefully as if protecting vases. The nuns shall not be allowed to travel, and without the blessing of the abbot, they shall not seek an opportunity of kissing or talking with men.[2] If they do otherwise, they must be subject to the penalties of the Rule.

Chapter 17

When an occasion presents itself that an abbot or monk from the men's monastery go to a women's monastery, the custom is not to greet the nuns individually, but that the abbess shall greet them first, and then the whole congregation. This applies to monks who come from a distance, not to those who live in the region nearby. When it is time to return to their own cells, the monks shall go to greet the abbess, and then all her nuns together, just as before. On these two occasions of entering and leaving, we allow permission to greet one another, but not otherwise, and even this must be with great modesty and restraint, as if Christ, the common Lord of both and the Bridegroom of the nuns, had come to

---

1 Sr. Clare Nock's interpretation of the Latin *carpentarii*.
2 *Viris* might refer to the husbands they had before the family entered the monastery.

stand in judgment and in the flesh. Christ is jealous, He does not want his house to be a house of procurers.[1] Further, we command this custom to be followed: that if the monks and nuns are brought together in one assembly to hear the words of salvation, the nuns may not sit next to the men, but each sex shall sit in separate groups. No abbot or brother shall henceforth, on any occasion, presume to kiss a sister[2] without the permission of the elders, nor to lay his head in the bosom of a nun as if by design; nor shall any woman dare to place her hands on the head or clothing of a monk to smooth it out. If a monk, whether from a distance or from the same monastery, fall ill, he may not lie down in the women's monastery, lest his mind become ill when his body is healed. As the blessed Jerome says: "He is a dangerous servant, if you are always watching what he wears."[3] For this reason, we command all sick monks to lie in the men's monastery and we further command that no woman shall minister to a man in his illness, whether mother or sister or wife or daughter or relative or no relative or maidservant, but if one of the above should be sent by the abbess with a bit of broth, they may not visit him, nor remain near him, except in the presence of the one whose duty is to minister to the sick. The same holds for men visiting women. No man shall rely upon chastity in the past, for none whose hearts are tainted by women can become holier than David or wiser than Solomon. That none may assume that his chastity is safe in the presence of a woman related to him, let him remember how Thamar was corrupted by her brother Amnon when he pretended to be ill.[4] Accordingly, both monks and nuns should live so chastely that they may have a good report, not only before God, but also before men, and may leave to those who follow an example of sanctity.

---

1 Cf. John 2.16.
2 Reading *sorori* for *seniori*.
3 Jerome, *Letter* 52.5.5 (CSEL 54.423) with *vultum* for *cultum*.
4 Cf. 2 Kings 13.

Chapter 18

We have learned that, in some less observant monasteries,
men have entered and brought their capital with them and
later, losing their religious fervor, have made great trouble
in demanding their property; and returning to the world
which they had left, as dogs return to their vomit,[1] with the
aid of their relatives have extorted what they had brought with
them to the monastery, and have sought the support of secular
judges and with the help of magistrates[2] have destroyed the
monasteries, so that we see many innocent men ruined by a
single sinner. Therefore, extreme precautions must be taken
in advance and every degree of discernment must be employed
to keep such from being received, since they come, not for
the love of Christ, but frightened by the approach of death
and forced by the inconvenience of bodily infirmity; not inspired by the desire for heaven, but merely frightened by the
punishment of hell. Of such the apostle says: "And he who
fears is not perfected in love; but perfect love casts out fear,
because fear brings punishment."[3] Such are not disciples of
Christ and are not to be sought in the Church, but are to be
found in the members of Antichrist; they are not "dwellers
in the land of good promise nor true Israelites,"[4] but proselytes
and strangers from afar; they are not faithful to the brothers,
nor strong in battle. In Leviticus, we learn that the Lord
hated such and forbade them to go to war, saying: "Let him
return home, lest he make his fellows as fainthearted as himself."[5] Of such, Verity says in the Gospel: "With difficulty
will a rich man enter the kingdom of heaven."[6] None of his
former possessions, not even so much as the smallest coin,

---

1 Cf. Prov. 26.11; 2 Peter 2.22.
2 Reading *saionibus* for *senioribus*.
3 1 John 4.18.
4 Cf. Heb. 11.9.
5 Cf. Deut. 20.8, not Leviticus.
6 Matt. 19.23.

should be received by the monastery into which he seeks
entrance; but he shall, with his own hands, bestow all his
goods on the poor, and then, when approved, shall be received
in the monastery under the Rule and for a full year shall be
specially tested by taunts from all the brothers. And when
he has been shown obedient in all things, not soft by nature
like lead, but hard as steel in endurance, then he may shed
his worldly garments and be clothed with the poor, simple
garments of the monastery and may be enrolled in the pact
with the brothers and may live among the monks, himself a
well-tried monk.

Chapter 19

First of all, we hope that those who have committed more
serious faults and failings will become submissive to the Rule
under the charge of a well-proved abbot and work with effort
in a monastery and will reveal all their former sins to a spiritual elder, just as the sick do to a doctor; and will, since they
have publicly sinned, publicly repent and not again commit
deeds needing repentance; will show fear of punishment,
love of the Kingdom, and hope for mercy; and will never
despair, for it is only at the end of life that justification or
condemnation is achieved. For it is written: "He himself
shall judge the ends of the earth."[1] The Lord justifies or condemns each man at the end, and considers the outcome of
all things, so that not even the sinner, if he truly repents, need
despair of forgiveness, nor should the just man have confidence
in his own sanctity. It is of no advantage to be dragged down
from the throne, to be deprived of royal power, to be bound
in irons and thrown in prison this very day; no more is it a
disadvantage if today one is released from prison and granted
royal honors. No one blames him for the sordidness of his
prison, but praises him for his admirable qualities. Just so,

---

1 1 Kings 2.10.

it is of no advantage to the just man to live well and to end
his life badly, and, likewise, it is a great good for a sinner to
repent, to have lived badly once, to have ended well later, to
have his past sins not charged against him by anyone. We
are sure that a judge rewards or condemns a man according
as he finds him at the end. Though his sins be great, he need
not for that reason lose hope of God's mercy. We know for
certain that publicans and sinners who had no previous merits
and were reserved for punishment in the court of justice have,
by the generous mercy of God, been redeemed after a brief
penance. In their case, however, it is not so much the length
of time as the extent of their repentance. Accordingly, each
one is to perform penance worthy of the severity of his sins,
so that if a man knows that he is guilty of any crime, it is
necessary, first of all, to judge that crime according to canon
law. It is written in the civil law that any guilty person who
has injured another party or committed murder or caused
damage may have his fine reduced by the judge, at whose
discretion it may be brought down from the original large
sum of money, lest some powerful person harm one who is
oppressed, so that one who legally was required to pay one
hundred coins may have the amount reduced to one-third,
as is written in the law books concerning those who are free.
Certainly, when we were slaves to sin, God had mercy on us
and we were freed by His justice, though possessed of no
previous good deeds; the debt of our sinfulness will be weighed
in the judgment of the most merciful judge in proportion to
the innumerable multitude of our sins. We realize that a
steward is put over us in proportion to the hundredfold weight
of the sins of our iniquity, who instead of one hundred jars
of oil will collect eighty; instead of one hundred bushels of
wheat, fifty, with the debt lessened. He immediately recognized that he was praised by his own master.[2] There are several who enter the monastery who would, according to the

---

2 Cf. Luke 16.1-8.

holy canons, be obliged to do penance outside the Church and
to receive communion only at the very end of their lives
because of their countless sins; we, however, who have learned
the mercy of the Lord and have been consoled, though lacking
in faith, reduce their many years to a brief number, lest they
perish in despair under the restraint of excessive sadness;
and we grant the reconciliation just as soon as we know that
they are deeply immersed in penance and humility. Even a
doctor lets his patient escape an operation if he thinks the
sick man can be cured by medicine. We allow them to have
food which will not inspire greater appetite nor hurt the body
too much. We forbid them to have meat, beer, or wine, but if
one of these seems to be necessary because of weakness or advanced old age, we leave it in the power and authority of the
elders. We offer them garments of sackcloth to wear, that the
rough goats' hair will constantly remind them that they stand
at the left hand of God to be judged for their sins.[3] We order
them to cover their bed with a skin or with a rush mat, which
in Latin is called *storea,* or if they have none of these, then,
with thin straw, except for those who are weak from illness
or age, as the abbots may determine for their comfort. You
may be sure that each one who observes what we have written
above will arrive at true moral health by worthy penance,
not by feigned humility. Amen.

Chapter 20

When any monk wrongly runs away from a monastery, he
must not be received into another community, nor shown any
kindness nor granted the kiss of peace, but must immediately
be brought back to his own abbot with his hands tied behind
his back. Or if he has returned to the world and, with the

---

3 Following the *Concordia* text in the interpretation of several very
obscure passages throughout this chapter.

help of his relatives, has risen to a position of insolence or threatens the monastery, then, both he and they are to be publicly expelled from the gatherings of the laity and are to remain anathematized from every gathering of Christians. If the laity also join with him and help him to stir flames of hatred against the monastery, they must all be driven out of the Church in shame and must not associate in any bonds of friendship with us, until they recognize the truth and stand on our side and help to vindicate the Church with a devotion equal to their previous hatred. If the apostates are driven away by all, and wander here and there unsettled and constantly on the move, and from sheer necessity desire to return to their monastery, they shall be brought to an assembly of the elders and tried like potter's vases in the furnace,[1] and when proved, they may be taken back to their monastery, but must sit in the lowest rank, not the highest.

---

1 Cf. Sirach (Ecclus.) 27.6.

PACT

I N THE NAME OF the Holy Trinity, Father and Son and Holy Spirit.

What we believe in our heart, we profess also with our mouth. We believe in the Father unborn, the Son born, and the Holy Spirit proceeding from both, that the Son alone received flesh from the Virgin and descended into the world for the salvation of all who believe in Him and that He never left the Father and the Holy Spirit. For He Himself said: "I and the Father are one."[1] And: "Who has me also has the Father." And: "Who sees me also sees the Father."[2] The same also said: "The heavens are my throne, the earth is my footstool."[3] In heaven, the angels worship the whole Trinity, and on earth, the Lord preaches to men, saying: "Go, sell all that thou hast and give to the poor, and come, follow me."[4] And again: "If anyone wishes to come after me, let him deny himself, and take up his cross, and follow me."[5] And elsewhere: "He who loves his father or mother, wife, children, or all the things that perish with the world, more than me, is not worthy of me."[6] And again: "Who does not hate his soul for my sake is not worthy of me."[7] And: "He who loses it for my sake will find it in eternal life."[8] So it is better, far better, to contemn the world, to listen to Christ,

---

1 John 10.30.
2 Cf. John 14.9.
3 Isa. 66.1; Acts 7.49.
4 Matt. 19.21; Luke 12.33.
5 Matt. 16.24; Luke 9.23.
6 Matt. 10.37; Luke 14.26.
7 Cf. Matt. 10.37; Luke 9.24.
8 Matt. 16.25; Luke 17.33; John 12.25.

to fulfill the Gospel, to possess a blessed life with the holy
angels forever through all ages. Thus, fired with divine ardor,
lo, all of us whose names are subscribed below entrust our
souls to God and to you, our master and our father, that we
may live in one monastery under Christ's guidance and your
teaching according to the edict of the apostles and the Rule,
and as sanctioned by the holy authority of the fathers in the
past. Whatever you desire for the safety of our souls to pro-
nounce, teach, perform, reprimand, command, excommunicate, or correct in accordance with the Rule, we shall completely carry out with humble heart, all arrogance aside, with
mind intent, with burning zeal, with the aid of divine grace,
without making excuses, and with the Lord's favor. If any
of us shall be complaining, obstinate, disobedient, or slander-
ing against the Rule and against your command, then, you
may have the power to bring all into an assembly and to read
the Rule in the presence of all and to correct our guilt publicly, and each one who is guilty shall receive his due, the lash
or ban of excommunication, with due consideration for his
misconduct. If anyone shall secretly intrigue with his parents, brothers, sons, relatives, or neighbors, or especially with
a fellow brother in the absence of the above-mentioned
father, you may have the power over each one who has attempted such a crime to have him put under ban of excommunication and confined to a dark cell for six months on
bread and water alone, wearing a penitential tunic or sackcloth, without cincture and without shoes. If a monk is
unwilling to undertake such penance with full consent, he is
to be stretched out naked and given 72 blows with a lash, and
to be deprived of the clothing of the monastery and to be
expelled from the institution in conspicuous disgrace, wearing
the clothes that he brought with him when he entered, but
torn. And this we declare both for men and for women.
We also promise to God and to you, our father, that if anyone through sinfulness goes anywhere else to live without

the blessing of the brothers and your consent, you may have the power to pursue the imprudent will of any monk who has tried such a thing, and to seize him and bring him before the judges[9] and of returning him to the censure of the Rule: and if any bishop or any of his own order or any layman desires to defend him and, in spite of hearing your warning, desires to keep the offender in his house, his association shall be with the devil and his communion with Judas Iscariot in hell; and in the present world, he shall be excommunicated from all Christian gatherings, and not even at the end of his life may such receive Extreme Unction. We remind you, our master, that if you should treat any of us unjustly—which it is unreasonable to believe and which may God not allow to happen—if you should treat any of us with pride or anger, or should love one and show hatred and rancor for another, or should dominate one but revere another, as people often do, then we shall have the right also granted to us by God to take our complaint without pride and without anger through the dean to the prior, and the prior shall humbly kiss the feet of you our lord and lay before you the details of our complaint, and you must be willing to listen patiently and to bend your neck humbly to the common Rule and correct and reform yourself. If you are not willing to correct yourself, then we may also have the power of consulting other monasteries, or else a bishop who lives under the Rule, or a Catholic count who is a defender of the Church, and of inviting them to meet with us, that, in their presence, you may correct yourself and fulfill the tenets of the Rule. We must be as your disciples, subjects, or adopted children, humble, obedient in all necessary things; and when we die you must offer us to Christ spotless and unharmed. Amen.

Here follow the names which each one, male or female, has subscribed to this pact with his or her own hand or sign.

---

9 Reading *saionibus* for *senioribus*.

LETTER OF FRUCTUOSUS TO KING RECESWINTH AND HIS BISHOPS ON BEHALF OF THE GUILTY WHO HAVE BEEN HELD IN PRISON SINCE THE TIME OF CHINTILA.[1]

FEAR THAT BY WRITING to you frequently I may increase your majesty's distaste, but I am more hesitant that by silence I may cause certain parties to lose your clemency—and may God never allow that to happen. Mindful of the words of the apostle, who said: "Have I then become your enemy, because I tell you the truth?"[2], I do not even tremble at the invectives and hostilities of your indignation, especially since I know the extremely clement attitude of your serene highnesses, not swollen with pride, but rather most considerate in the practices of Christian compassion and the teachings of our Lord, continuously filled to overflowing with sentiments of commiseration, and always anxious to perform what may be of common benefit to all in misery.

In my wretched unworthiness, O most pious lord, I presume to ask that you not allow your good reputation for justice to be infringed. Long since the reward of your generosity and pity have been solidly won and established in the presence of the Lord; bestow a suitable gift on the unfortunate through the benevolence of your piety and do not in any way deprive of your generosity any person, however guilty, but let your good will, which is accustomed

---

1 This last name is *Scindani* in the manuscripts, emended by editors to *Sisenandi*. I follow K. Zeumer in *Neues Archiv*, 2nd ser., 24 (1899) 66 n., who proposes *Scindilani*, a variant of *Chintilani*. Actually the decree of Chindaswinth concerning rebellious subjects is made retroactive to the time of Chintila (cf. *Leges Visigothorum* 2.1.6). Otherwise this title agrees with the Escorial manuscript, except for omitting the *Domnus* before each of the proper names.
2 Gal. 4.16.

to spare its adversaries, overcome the evil dispositions of men and show leniency to those about to die, with the favor of Christ the Lord.

"Forgive and you shall be forgiven."[3] Do not let the fear of profanation close the heart of your serene highnesses to being willing to spare; for in this you may wash away the martyrdoms caused by your father[4] and the spots of your own sins, if, with the favor of Christ the Lord, you check the punishment of the wretched and remove the bonds of their chains. It is useless to put forth an oath as an excuse for an impious act, when it is clearly proved to be contrary to the words of Christ; there is no faith where love of good works and mercy are lacking: "If you do not," says the Lord, "forgive your brothers from your hearts, neither will your heavenly Father forgive your offenses."[5]

He who truly desires to expiate himself of his own sin must forgive another, and since none may boast that he has a clean heart, and the conscience of no man upon earth, however just, is free from sins, why should one try to add perfidy to cruelty? And since it is commanded to forgive one's enemies,[6] I wonder how those who by cruelty are involved in such afflictions will be able to overcome cruelty by the infliction of seclusion and confinement upon the vanquished. If an impious oath makes it impossible to show mercy, then it is extremely cruel that the patronage of indulgence is denied to your royal and priestly clemency. If you follow such counsel, my lord sincerely and especially beloved by me next to God, and you most venerated and holy fathers and bishops of your servant, what will God think, when, as judge of the universe, He shall come to judge the world with fire. You must consider that.

---

3 Luke 6.37.
4 Chindaswinth became king in 642 and his early policies were quite violent.
5 Cf. Matt. 18.35; Matt. 6.15.
6 Cf. Matt. 5.44.

May He in His piety grant that your serene highnesses may so conduct this case that you may win, not the stamp of condemnation, but eternal glory.

MONASTIC AGREEMENT

(Consensoria monachorum)

INTRODUCTION

The *Consensoria Monachorum*[1] is a form of monastic pact, intended for use with some type of *Rule,* just as the *Pact* already translated was attached to the *Common Rule,* attributed to Fructuosus. It was a legal agreement to be subscribed with the signatures of the monks. A full account of the title, contents, and unique nature of the *Consensoria* has been given by Professor Bishko, who assigns it to Galicia in the years 650-675. It contains references to the armed violence experienced in that area when abbeys were attacked by kinsmen seeking to recover property donated by a relative when he professed monasticism.

The biblical quotations were made from an Old Latin version rather than from the Vulgate. One citation in Chapter 3 from prophetic literature seems to be apocryphal.

This translation is based on the text in PL 66.993-996 and on variants indicated in the notes from another version edited in an appendix to works of Augustine in PL 32.1447-1450 as well as other manuscript readings printed by Bishko. There are more recent editions by A. C. Vega, *La regla de San Agustín* (El Escorial 1933), and R. Arbesmann and W. Hümpfner, *Iordani de Saxonia Liber Vitasfratrum* (New York 1943) 485-88.

---

1 Listed as no. 1872 in Dekkers, *Clavis patrum latinorum.*

SELECT BIBLIOGRAPHY

Bishko, C. J. "The Date and Nature of the Spanish *Consensoria Mona-chorum*," *American Journal of Philology* 69 (1948) 377-95.

Migne, J. P. *Patrologiae latinae cursus completus* (Paris 1844-1864) 32, 66 (=PL).

MONASTIC AGREEMENT

(*Consensoria Monachorum*)[1]

(1) By common agreement we have decreed among ourselves what shall never be infringed by anyone hereafter. In the name of our Lord Jesus Christ, we who reside in the monastery have all agreed, in accordance with apostolic tradition, to have one opinion and to hold possessions in common, as it is written: "By thinking alike in the Lord."[2] No one shall claim anything as his own, but as it is written in the Acts of the Apostles: "Holding all things in common, and no one said that anything he possessed was his own,"[3] which was also written for us. Accordingly, let us hold ourselves in the Lord under the terms of monastic agreement and civil law, and let us abide in these rules until the end, for it is written: "He who has persevered to the end will be saved."[4]

(2) If anyone desires to join a congregation of brothers who are in agreement, let him not ignore the saying of the Gospel: "Let him sell all that he has and bestow it on the needy and poor."[5] And again: "Let him deny himself, and take up his cross, and follow Christ."[6] Let him not be anxious in his heart for food and clothing and other things which are necessary for the body, for the Lord Himself in the Gospels forewarns in these words: "Do not be anxious, saying, 'What shall you eat?' or, 'What shall you put on?' (for after

---

1 *Consensoria* is found nowhere else, but Prof. Bishko plausibly interprets it as a noun with essentially the same meaning as *pactum, placitum,* or *definitio.*
2 Cf. Phil. 2.2.
3 Acts 4.32.
4 Matt. 10.22.
5 Cf. Matt. 19.21.
6 Cf. Luke 9.23.

these things the Gentiles seek); for your Father knows that
you need all these things. Seek the kingdom of God and his
justice, and all these things shall be given you besides."[7]

(3) But before he decides to remain in the monastery, he
must approve the purpose and example of the brothers, and
he must himself be approved in all his conduct by the one
who is the prior and by the agreement of the rest, for the
sake of the teaching and advice of the prophet: "Do not be
quick to commend a friend, or if you have commended him
quickly, do not be quick to reprove."[8]

(4) If anyone shall be removed from the monastery for
any necessary reason, he shall not even think of taking away
with him any of the things that are in the monastery, or of
those things which he formerly brought with him, or of those
things which he acquired while with the brothers,[9] for it is
agreed that the brothers may not hold, possess, give, or
receive anything without the permission of the superior.
If a neighbor or friend or any of the brothers wishes to
offer anything, it is first necessary to inform the prior; then
it may be accepted, if he approves, but nothing may be done
except what is pleasing to the prior or allowed by him,
since it is much to be feared that he may experience exactly
what is written: "He who has no guard on his speech shall
bring downfall."[10] Again, he shall by no means incite any
of the brothers to go with him, lest he be judged more a de-
stroyer than a builder of the monastery, because of which
there is written: "He who is not with me is against me, and
he who does not gather with me scatters."[11] Anyone who is
incited by another to leave the monastery must either rebuke
the inciter or inform the abbot, who may not fail to observe
any of those things which we have decided together, for it is

---

7 Matt. 6.31-33.
8 Only the first phrase is in PL; the rest is from a manuscript reading
   in Bishko, *op. cit.* The quotation is probably apocryphal.
9 Long omission due to homoeoteleuton supplied from PL 32.1459.
10 Cf. Prov. 13.3.
11 Matt. 12.30.

written: "Be at peace with many, but let one in a thousand be your confidant."[12]

(5) What is written here shall be observed constantly and with all diligence from the abbot to all the brothers. If anyone hears from another, one in whom he believes, an ascetic practice different from that which is followed in the monastery, he shall both refuse to accept the practice and shall make it known to the leader of the monks, for it is written: "All that is made manifest is light."[13] If the teachings are found good, they must be approved; if false, they must be corrected.

(6) If one of the brothers who agreed upon a common pact shall suddenly on one occasion only[14] fall into altercation with another, he may, according to the Gospel, ask and receive forgiveness;[15] but if he refuses to mend his ways, and if the one against whom a wrong has been done has not succeeded in changing the other's presumption after a first and second admonishment, then he shall report it to the abbot, lest both he and his brother be endangered by this silence; as the prophet says: "He who hides his enmity maintains deceit."[16]

(7) If, as often happens, a sudden invasion or attack of the enemy takes place,[17] so that it is impossible for the brothers to seek flight together because of the pursuit of their enemies, and if later they escape with God's help and shall be able to go wherever they have learned that the abbot is, they must hasten thither as sons to a father. Nor can they ever be

---

12 Cf. Sirach (Ecclus.) 6.6.
13 Eph. 5.13.
14 Text modified from PL 32.
15 Cf. Matt. 18.15-17.
16 Cf. Prov. 26.24.
17 Bishko interprets this hostility as referring to the *Common Rule*, p. 202 above, where several provisions are made in case the relatives and family of a monk try to recover by force the property which he has brought to the monastery.

separated once the divine love has joined them, for we are advised: "Perfect love casts out fear."[18]

(8) If anyone, as we have said above, for any necessary reason shall possess something which he has carried with him from the monastery, he must take it where his abbot is, since he will not be able to retain as his own what belongs to all according to the Pact and has accordingly been consecrated to God. If he contemplates retaining any of these things, he seems to be contradicting the words of the apostle, who said: "Owe no man anything except to love one another."[19]

(9) All the brothers who[20] desire to be one in the Lord shall observe all the things that are written in this book,[21] and shall subscribe their names. These precautions have not[22] been taken on behalf of those who are known to be steadfast in all things.

---

18 1 John 4.18.
19 Rom. 13.8.
20 Reading *qui* from PL 32 for *quia*.
21 Following Bishko, the "book" would probably be this *Consensoria* plus a *Rule* (Basilian or Isidorian) to which it was attached.
22 Adding *non* from an Escorial manuscript (cf. Bishko, *op. cit.* 387-88).

INDICES

GENERAL INDEX

abbots, 167, 168, 170-173, 181, 182, 185, 187, 190-192; allegiance to, 152; appointment of, 36-38; duties of, 193, 195-198; resignation of, 36-38.

Abraham, 106-108.

Abundantius, senator, 136.

Acephalites, heresy of, 142.

Achab, 72.

Achaz, 109.

Acts of the Apostles, 217.

Adam, 193.

ad aurem, 38 n.

Aesop, 30.

Agar the Egyptian, 97, 106-108.

Agivarius, 68 n.

Alexandria, 57 n.

Almighty, will of, 43.

altar, covering of on Good Friday, 40.

Amen, 39.

amicitia, 16 n.

amictus, 16 n.

amitto, 68 n.

Amnon, 201.

Ananias, 121, 164, 180, 183.

Anatolius of Laodicea, 58 n.

angels, 207.

anger, 124.

Anianus, bishop of Valencia, 60 n.

Anthony, St., 124.

Antichrist, 111, 180, 202; demons of, 55.

anti-Jewish sentiment, 51 n.

anti-Priscillianism, 111 n.

Apicella, 43.

Apocalypse, Commentary of Apringius, 64, 65.

apostles, 192; desert their duty, 39; relics of, 27, 28.

Apostolic See, 54.

Appius, 32, 34.

Apringius, bishop of Beja, *Commentary on the Apocalypse,* 64, 65.

Aquitania, 45 n.

Arbesmann, R., 215.

Arevalo, F., 10 n.

Arles, 98 n.

armatura, 32 n.

Armentarius, monk cured by St. Emilian, 116, 125, 126.

Asellus, priest, 136.

ass, 87, 118.

Astorga, 102 n., 111 n., 147.

Ataulfus, 67.

Audax, bishop of Tarragona, 25 n.

Augustine, St., 6, 10, 27, 89

223

INDEX TO HOLY SCRIPTURE

(Books of the Old Testament)

James
    1.11: 49
    1.17: 59, 60
    2.13: 42
    5.16: 100

1 Peter
    1.24: 49
    2.23: 32
    4.10: 21, 22

2 Peter
    2.22: 202

1 John
    4.8: 29
    4.16: 23, 102
    4.18: 24, 139, 202, 220

Apocalypse (Revelation)
    2.9: 31

THE FATHERS OF THE
CHURCH SERIES

(A series of approximately 100 volumes when completed)

ADVANTAGE OF BELIEVING (trans. by Sr. Luanne
Meagher)
ON FAITH IN THINGS UNSEEN (trans. by Deferrari
and Sr. Mary Francis McDonald)

VOL. 5: ST. AUGUSTINE (1948)
THE HAPPY LIFE (trans. by Schopp)
ANSWER TO SKEPTICS (trans. by Kavanagh)
DIVINE PROVIDENCE AND THE PROBLEM OF EVIL
(trans. by Russell)
SOLILOQUIES (trans. by Gilligan)

VOL. 6: ST. JUSTIN MARTYR (1948)
FIRST AND SECOND APOLOGY (trans. by Falls)
DIALOGUE WITH TRYPHO (trans. by Falls)
EXHORTATION AND DISCOURSE TO THE GREEKS
(trans. by Falls)
THE MONARCHY (trans. by Falls)

VOL. 7: NICETA OF REMESIANA (1949)
WRITINGS (trans. by Walsh and Monohan)
SULPICIUS SEVERUS
WRITINGS (trans. by Peebles)
VINCENT OF LERINS
COMMONITORIES (trans. by Morris)
PROSPER OF AQUITANE
GRACE AND FREE WILL (trans. by O'Donnell)

VOL. 8: ST. AUGUSTINE (1950)
CITY OF GOD, Bks. I-VII (trans. by Walsh, Zema;
introduction by Gilson)

VOL. 9: ST. BASIL (1950)
ASCETICAL WORKS (trans. by Sr. M. Monica
Wagner)

VOL. 10: TERTULLIAN (1950)
APOLOGETICAL WORKS (vol. 1), (trans. by Arbes-
mann, Sr. Emily Joseph Daly, Quain)
MINUCIUS FELIX
OCTAVIUS (trans. by Arbesmann)

VOL. 11: ST. AUGUSTINE (1951)
COMMENTARY ON THE LORD'S SERMON ON THE
MOUNT WITH SEVENTEEN RELATED SERMONS
(trans. by Kavanagh)

245

VOL. 42: ST. AMBROSE (1961)
HEXAMERON, PARADISE, AND CAIN AND ABEL (trans. by Savage)

VOL. 43: PRUDENTIUS (1962)
POEMS (vol. 1), (trans. by Sr. M. Clement Eagan)

VOL. 44: ST. AMBROSE (1963)
THEOLOGICAL AND DOGMATIC WORKS (trans. by Deferrari)

VOL. 45: ST. AUGUSTINE (1963)
THE TRINITY (trans. by McKenna)

VOL. 46: ST. BASIL (1963)
EXEGETIC HOMILIES (trans. by Sr. Agnes Claré Way)

VOL. 47: ST. CAESARIUS OF ARLES (1964)
SERMONS 81-186 (vol. 2), (trans. by Sr. Mary Magdeleine Mueller)

VOL. 48: ST. JEROME (1964)
HOMILIES 1-59 (vol. 1), (trans. by Sr. Marie Liguori Ewald)

VOL. 49: LACTANTIUS (1964)
THE DIVINE INSTITUTES, Bks. I-VII (trans. by Sr. Mary Francis McDonald)

VOL. 50: OROSIUS (1964)
SEVEN BOOKS AGAINST THE PAGANS (trans. by Deferrari)

VOL. 51: ST. CYPRIAN (1965)
LETTERS (trans. by Sr. Rose Bernard Donna)

VOL. 52: PRUDENTIUS (1965)
POEMS (vol. 2), (trans. by Sr. M. Clement Eagan)

VOL. 53: ST. JEROME (1965)
DOGMATIC AND POLEMICAL WORKS (trans. by John N. Hritzu)

VOL. 54: LACTANTIUS (1965)
THE MINOR WORKS (trans. by Sr. Mary Francis McDonald)

VOL. 55: EUGIPPIUS (1965)
LIFE OF ST. SEVERIN (trans. by Bieler)

VOL. 56: ST. AUGUSTINE (1966)
THE CATHOLIC AND MANICHAEAN WAYS OF LIFE
(trans. by Donald A. and Idella J. Gallagher)

VOL. 57: ST. JEROME (1966)
HOMILIES 60-96 (vol. 2), (trans. by Sr. Marie
Liguori Ewald)

VOL. 58: ST. GREGORY OF NYSSA (1966)
ASCETICAL WORKS (trans. by Virginia Woods
Callahan)

VOL. 59: ST. AUGUSTINE (1968)
THE TEACHER, THE FREE CHOICE OF THE WILL,
GRACE AND FREE WILL (trans. by Russell)

VOL. 60: ST. AUGUSTINE (1968)
THE RETRACTATIONS (trans. by Sr. Mary Inez
Bogan)

VOL. 61: ST. CYRIL OF JERUSALEM, VOL. 1 (1969)
PROCATECHESIS, CATECHESES 1-12 (trans. by Mc-
Cauley and Stephenson)

VOL. 62: IBERIAN FATHERS, VOL. 1 (1969)
MARTIN OF BRAGA, PASCHASIUS OF DUMIUM,
LEANDER OF SEVILLE (trans. by Barlow)

VOL. 63: IBERIAN FATHERS, VOL. 2 (1969)
BRAULIO OF SARAGOSSA, FRUCTUOSUS OF BRAGA
(trans. by Barlow)